DISCIPLINE

THE MOST IMPORTANT SUBJECT WE TEACH

Robert L. Major

UNIVERSITY
PRESS OF
AMERICA

Lanham • New York • London

Copyright © **1990 by**
University Press of America®, Inc.
4720 Boston Way
Lanham, Maryland 20706

3 Henrietta Street
London WC2E 8LU England

Library of Congress Cataloging-in-Publication Data

Major, Robert L., 1940–   .
Discipline, the most important subject we teach / Robert L. Major.
p.   cm.
Includes bibliographical references.
1. School discipline—United States.   2. Discipline of children—
United States.   3. Rewards and punishments in education.
4. Classroom management—United States.   I. Title.
LB3012.2.M35   1990   371.5'0973—dc20   89–70745 CIP

ISBN 0–8191–7745–8 (alk. paper)

™ The paper used in this publication meets the minimum requirements of
American National Standard for Information Sciences—Permanence
of Paper for Printed Library Materials, ANSI Z39.48–1984.

To Verta A. Major,

a great teacher and mother.

She would have enjoyed this book.

ACKNOWLEDGMENTS

I had an outstanding teacher in every education course I took, from the bachelor's level through the doctorate. I'm the only person I know who can say this. To all of you at the University of Northern Colorado, Teachers College Columbia University, and the University of Nebraska, thank you for setting high standards and for making me write, think, read, and feel good about myself.

Also, thank you, students; especially those in my discipline and classroom management classes. Your honesty and openness helped me learn as much as you. You will see your thinking, ideas, contributions and advice on most every page. Again, thank you.

TABLE OF CONTENTS

CHAPTER

Preface

Communities exist today where people help stranded motorists, feed the less fortunate, and accept smiles at face value. People living there believe a person's word means something and settle agreements with a handshake.

This sort of community may make you think, "Oh, goody, can the Beaver come out to play?"; yet, wouldn't it be nice to escape, at least occasionally, rude, inconsiderate, and boorish behavior? You know, giggling in the library when you are trying to study, loud music and boisterous behavior when you are trying to think, and vulgarity on streets when your parents are with you.

When you read about nurses being raped in hospital parking lots, the elderly getting mugged for their Social Security checks, and 45% of our population restricting its daily behavior out of fear (Moore & Trojanowicz, 1988, p. 3), don't you sometimes think the world has gone a bit mad--that the bullies, predators, and misfits are controlling the majority? Oh, to live where people do not intrude on others and show respect for one another!

This idea is hardly unique, nor is it particularly realistic, but I believe such a society can be created and that this creation can occur without that society becoming one where people mind everyone's business but their own, believe they are the only ones with correct values, put down anyone who is different, and gossip like men in a barbershop.

I know the rich have gotten richer and the poor have gotten poorer (the top 20% in wealth earned nine times more than the poorest in 1986, up from seven times as much in 1979) (U.S. Bureau of Labor Statistics, 1988, p. 16A), that racism is still very much alive, and that "good old boy" clubs which exclude and demean outsiders still exist; but in spite of this, I believe a polite, well-mannered society that respects individuality can exist.

It can if our country's brightest and best become teachers! That is because teachers control everyone during the most formative years of life. Dictators have always understood this and have treated youth as their country's most valuable resource. Teachers have power. And this power, for good or for evil, is there just for the taking.

Why aren't our brightest, most sensitive, most honest, and best already teachers? We both know--pitiful salaries, mean-spirited parents, bad press, no respect from anyone, and, in some cases, pathetic administrators. It takes courage to be a teacher. It takes ignoring a lot of imbeciles, re-sensitizing oneself to what's important, learning to function almost entirely on intrinsic motivation, and demonstrating full maturity before one is ready to be that mature.

This book is written for those of you who believe helping young children prepare for life in our complex society is a most-worthy goal; for those who believe that the only solid foundation for an education system is its teachers; for those who believe public schools are society's most genuine attempt to give every young person an equal chance of making the best of himself or herself; and for those who believe your own children and grandchildren deserve a better society than the one you got.

Each chapter can stand alone, but each chapter also contains a theme, which is, when it comes to discipline: attitudes, perceptions, and expectations mean everything. The attitudes you have about students, co-workers, parents, etc. determine your perceptions; and your perceptions determine your expectations; and your expectations determine what goes on in the classroom. This is so because nothing is truer in teaching than--"What a teacher expects is what a teacher gets."

This book focuses upon discipline rather than other worthy topics such as foundations of curriculum, learning styles, and improvement of instruction, because if you don't survive, you won't be around to create a new society. Without discipline, you have nothing.

Teaching is much too important and your mission too vital to allow the uncivilized few, the ill mannered, the poorly parented, to drive you out, thus robbing even those not yet born of perhaps the best teacher in the world.

References

Moore, Mark H., and Robert C. Trojanowicz. "Policing and the Fear of Crime." _Perspectives on Policing_. Washington, D.C.: Department of Justice, June 1988, no. 3, p. 3.

U.S. Bureau of Labor Statistics. _Sunday Omaha World-Herald_, 6 November 1988: 16A.

CHAPTER I

CRITICAL INCIDENTS IN TEACHING

Years ago, when Today's Education was called the N.E.A. Journal, there was always a section called "What Would You Do?" Teachers wrote about frustrations, usually incidents involving misbehaving students, and then a couple of experts or a self-proclaimed expert would reply.

For the past 10 years, I have asked my graduate students, most of whom are experienced teachers, to share their "Critical Incident in Teaching." I've included a sampling to help you anticipate the range of problems you might expect. If you can anticipate problems before you have to act, you are more apt to behave as a mature adult, which is how students expect you to behave, rather than an angry parent or spoiled child when these incidents occur.

Not included are incidents involving students calling teachers foul names, students making obscene gestures when teachers tell them what to do, or incidents involving the breaking up of fights. These incidents apparently happen so frequently, they should be expected going in. Before signing a contract, see what that school's handbook says about breaking up student fights, being hit by a student, handling children who refuse to follow your directives, and how teachers should react to getting cussed out. Remember, however, that teachers and administrators often ignore handbooks and adhere to guidelines not even mentioned. So, ask how those currently in charge handle fighting, obscenity, and disobedience.

Incidentally, teachers handle these things all the way from ignoring them through being deliberately slow to react, yelling commands, sending for help, and jumping right in and being physical. We don't know for sure how we will react until confronted by such situations. Because we don't, my advice is this: try not to react in kind; pride yourself in being the one person who can keep his cool; and know the person involved in the misdeeds must be in unbearable pain. If it is a fight, for gosh sakes, don't grab just one student who is fighting and hold them. The other combatant may just punch her out and there you are, holding a defenseless person, while the other is pounding on her.

1

Here, then, are 20 incidents. (Appendix "A" contains additional Critical Incidents.)

Incident #1

The first weekend of my first year of teaching, I was invited to a wedding party by the chairman of the school board. I had nothing to do, and I didn't know anyone in the town, so I went. I was the only teacher there, and I was taken by surprise when I saw 80% of my juniors and seniors drinking around a keg that was in the backyard. The football team and the volleyball team were all drinking, and here I was, a 22-year-old trying to figure out what to do. When school started the following Monday, I had a note to report to the superintendent's office, so I did. I don't know how he found out that I was there (chairman's party), but he did, and he asked me what I was going to do. I said that I really didn't know since this was my sixth day of teaching, so he recommended that we put all this "on the shelf" for the time being. I get pissed off every time I think about it.

Incident #2

I walked out one day in junior high sub-teaching after two hours and told the principal I couldn't handle the kids. It was a bad day to begin with; I'd never met them before. They poured water on me, threw spitballs, everything. Such a fiasco. I finally put down my pen and just stood there and said, "O.K., you win!," and never went back. I bet it had some kind of effect, though. I don't think I really lost, just kind of woke up to the fact that I counted more than that. Anyway, that's how I've coped with it.

Incident #3

A chemically dependent girl (she had been in treatment twice) came to school one morning exhibiting a lot of behaviors that were not normal for her--she was laughing, patting people on the back, being very outgoing. After about a half-hour, she came to the staff--there are three of us in an alternative school-- and said she had taken 40 pills on her way to school. She wanted to know what would happen to her. At first, we didn't believe her, but then, she fainted. After she was in the hospital, we learned that her "friends" had watched, encouraged, and even counted the pills for her that morning. We then had to deal with their attitudes and her re-entry into the school.

Incident #4

A girl was continually disrupting my class by arguing with other students, with what I was teaching, with the color of the blackboard, anything and everything. I called her mother to try to get help in resolving the issue. I was told that the girl's brother had committed suicide and that I should lay off and not bring stress into the girl's life or she might do the same.

Incident #5

I asked an eighth grade boy to come in after school to finish his work. He didn't come, so had to be sent for. He was very irritated by this, walked in, and slammed the door. He started yelling at me, saying I was too strict. He started his work, but wrote overly large. He alternated between standing up and yelling at me and continuing his writing. This went on for about a half an hour. I think I handled this correctly by refusing to react, defend myself, or return the anger. I simply sat at my desk and wrote down everything he said. When he finished his work, he came and apologized, saying, "I don't know why I act like that."

Incident #6

The teacher was keeping a boy after school for an hour for acting up during class. The teacher unlocked his walk-in closet and proceeded to get on a ladder to get some materials off the top shelf. At that point, the student decided he had been there long enough and locked the teacher in the closet and threw the key in the wastebasket. A janitor found the teacher in the closet three hours later and, after another hour, was able to get the teacher out of the closet when a key was found. I was the student. The teacher is now the superintendent, and I teach for him.

Incident #7

Last November, my colleagues and I played a volleyball match against the senior class--faculty versus students. Our purpose was none other than to have some fun. The seniors ended up winning two out of three, and after the crowd broke up, we all headed for

3

the parking lot. We got to the parking lot and found three egg cartons on the ground and, nearby, three teachers' cars covered with eggs. We just stood there in disbelief. Who would do such a thing? Why, after such a delightful evening, would someone vandalize our cars? After an investigation and after a number of suspects were questioned, we still had no answers; no one was ever caught or punished.

Incident #8

The principal in the school system gives direct consequences for behavior problems. After misbehavior by two sophomore students, the boys were taken into the school's locker room. They were asked to stand at opposite ends of the room and told to run headfirst into each other. One boy explained to his parents that the welt on his head was a reaction to a wasp's sting.

Incident #9

We were working on an extremely difficult math problem. I wanted to impress upon my seniors that it is important not to quit a problem just because they cannot solve the problem on the first try. My comment was, "If you play with it long enough, it will eventually come." I will never forget the uproar in my entire life.

Incident #10

This incident occurred in a senior high metal shop. A student, 12th grade, didn't think he needed to do anything. He kept going around bothering other people. I told him to sit down twice. The third time was close to the end of the period. I told him to stay after the bell rang. He did, and I took him in the tool room. The tool room has one door, no windows. Then, I asked him his problem and told him if he wants to smart off, now is the time. I then proceeded to tell him how much of a donkey he has been and what I expect out of him from now on. It worked. I didn't have any more problems with this student the rest of the quarter.

Incident #11

Having been away from teaching for 21 years, I don't have any recent experiences to draw from. However, I do remember very vividly what a disaster my

4

first year of teaching was. I had some unusually difficult children and lacked the training and skills necessary to know how to cope. I remember one little boy who sat in the front of the room (guess why?) and would write obscenities on his arm and hold it up for the rest of the class to see. Right before school would be out, he would ask to go to the washroom. When I discovered what he was up to, I told him he couldn't wash it off until his parents had seen it, and I wanted a note from them acknowledging they had. This did put an end to the problem, but the mother also informed me her son was not the only one doing things like this.

Incident #12

An incident from my first year of teaching in 1958 stands out in my memory. I was teaching in a small country parochial school with the lower four grades in my room. I stood next to a third grader as I reprimanded him. Turning around to continue teaching, I caught sight of him sticking his tongue out at me. I swung around and slapped him on the mouth. After my anger subsided, I regretted my action. The thought of how severely I could have injured the boy has stayed with me through all the years, so I never again slapped a child on the face or head.

Incident #13

During this school year, four of our students were involved in an incident in which an SLBP student was urinated on. The SLBP student cannot speak, so he could not tell what had happened to him, but his teacher could smell urine on him and he was wet up and down his body. His teacher reported her suspicions about what had happened to the administration. I think the administration was given a tip about four ninth grade boys who were supposed to have been in class at the time of the incident. When these students were questioned, two flatly denied any involvement. The other two admitted to watching the others urinate on the SLBP student.

Incident #14

I was the cheerleading advisor at my school. One day, one of my senior cheerleaders asked to talk to me in my office. She began her conversation with, "As you probably know, I'm pregnant." Well, I didn't know and was shocked, to say the least. In a matter-of-fact tone, she proceeded to tell me that she was two months pregnant, and that the doctor had told her she could continue to do whatever physical activity she had been doing, including cheerleading. I started to say that I didn't feel our athletic director and administration would allow a pregnant cheerleader and she may be asked to resign. (Now, for the bombshell.) She looked me square in the eye and said, "The father of this baby is playing on the basketball team and I will cheerlead . . . or I will see you in court!" She turned, opened the door, and left.

Incident #15

Once I got too carried away with the honesty issue. Someone in my classroom was missing $2.00. I questioned everyone in the class and put the "honest" kids through lots of torment. They felt so bad. I wanted to stress the importance of honesty and admitting to their errors. Instead, I made them feel that I didn't trust them. I blew it way out of proportion and had kids in tears. I handled this totally wrong.

Incident #16

During an art class, a few of the girls began screaming that they saw maggots and they (the maggots) were crawling all over the floor in that particular area. After moving a cart containing plaster, I saw a dead bird that had obviously been there a long time. The girls were screaming, the boys were quiet (very quiet).

Incident #17

In my classroom, I keep a seating chart and request that my students sit in assigned seats. One girl (this is a 10th grade math class) would sit in a different seat every day, and I would have to move her to her correct seat. One day when she walked into the room, I asked where she was going to sit for that period. She replied, "Where do you want me to sit, on your face?" I tried to ignore that remark as the class laughed, but awhile later, she swore at another student and I asked her to leave the room. In the end, she was dropped from my class with an "F."

Incident #18

This incident took place five years ago. I warned this child if he didn't stay in his chair while I was teaching a math lesson, I'd have to take the chair away from him. Unfortunately, the chair was removed from him and he had to stand by his desk and listen to the remaining lesson. The next morning, his mother came to school. She was very upset with me, yelling and screaming about the incident in front of my class and her son. After I told her the situation, she walked quietly out of the building. The entire year she was extremely nice to me.

Incident #19

I had noon hour supervision for high school students. Students were to use a certain stairway and not enter the elementary part of the school. One large senior boy ignored the rules routinely and stomped past, walking as loudly as he could in cowboy boots. He deliberately used the wrong stairs. He had been in chemical dependency treatment, had a less-than-pleasant home situation, and most teachers hated to hassle or cross him up over anything that was not of major importance--partly because of retaliation and partly because he was having a difficult period in his life. I finally engaged in casual conversation in the hall with him about non-school subjects, and soon he was using the right stairs--apparently no longer caring to defy me.

Incident #20

Scott was an above-average student who became a discipline problem because he said he was bored. Once the lesson had been presented and he understood it, he would become a clown to those around him. This did not hurt his learning, but those around him had a drop in test scores. Finally, his parents became involved when I contacted them because of missing homework and general fooling around. They were very concerned. Their approach was to visit the classroom every day for a week. This embarrassed Scott, but he did shape up. The parents asked to be informed if there was any back-sliding. The first time I called, they were at school within 10 minutes. I also spoke privately with Scott to reinforce his good points and try to show him how very much I cared for him as a person. We always had a friendly relationship, no matter how much it seemed I was "on his case." This happened last year. This year, he told a teacher that I was the one who helped him the most last year.

These incidents should start the thinking and help make the following chapters more meaningful. We will again encounter critical incidents in Chapter XIV, Role Playing and Discipline.

CHAPTER II

DISCIPLINE, THE MOST IMPORTANT SUBJECT WE TEACH

Discipline should be given as high a priority in our curriculum as we now give reading, writing, and arithmetic. This is a strong statement; but, before rejecting it, please scan the next paragraph--we will be reading a small-town newspaper.

In the local section, we learn a man is running around spraying acid on peoples' posteriors and that a live rabbit, stolen from the local zoo, was thrown from the fourth floor of the downtown parking ramp. (The fall, of course, made it splatter all over, upsetting those below.) In the state section, we learn three 14-year-old girls attempted to poison their assistant principal by putting iodine in his coffee (The Free Press, March 4, 1986, p. 13), and that a student used a baseball bat to beat up the teacher who gave him an F. And, in the national section, we discover a motorist, who stopped to help an abandoned crying baby that was sitting in the middle of a deserted road, in January, dressed only in a diaper and nightshirt, was attacked by two men. When she stopped, they rushed from the bushes, put a knife to her throat, stole $300.00 from her purse, and fled with the child (The Free Press, January 9, 1986); that a nine-year-old was stabbed and beaten to death by an 11-, a 12-, and a 14-year-old because he refused to share his bicycle (Minneapolis Star Tribune, August 7, 1985, p. 68); that police found a 30-year-old naked woman, covered with feces and being fed whole corn from a cut-off Clorox bottle, locked in a small room. She was just lying there mindlessly kicking the wall. She had been there for many years, and although the neighbors knew about it, they never called the authorities (The Free Press, May 7, 1985, p. 10); and that two teen-agers, after paying a 19-year-old $60.00 to kill their father, hid his body, cashed his paycheck, and used that money plus his credit cards to go on a $2,000.00 shopping spree (The Free Press, February 1979). Are the selfish and inconsiderate taking over?

Do the above incidents have anything to do with discipline being the most important subject we teach? In my mind, they do, because they are but the tip of the iceberg. Not included are incidents that occur so frequently they do not make the news: swearing on buses, robberies at interstate rest areas, barking dogs, loud parties, disobeyed leash laws, etc.

Discipline is the most important subject we teach, because without it, all of us will have to live in a society not fit for anyone--not even for those who can't or won't subject themselves to even a limited degree of conformity. Can we help students behave as civilized, reasonably well-mannered, decent human beings when we are not around? That, I believe, is the overriding question; how we answer it will determine the quality of life we all enjoy.

As educational leaders, as ones expected to discover standards and promote ideas for which society professes to have faith, are we doing all we can to graduate students who will at least get off their duffs and phone 911 when they see a woman being stabbed? No one in our lifetime or in our children's lifetime should ever again have to read about another infamous New York City stabbing incident of someone like Kitty Genovese.

How can we create this better society? The first step is to remember that not more than 10% of our students are responsible for most of the problems (National Institute of Education, 1978, p. 168); that our good works are not always overridden by elements outside the classroom; that when we react to discipline situations, we are modeling how students themselves might react when they are adults; and that many support us, including security personnel in malls, store owners, bus drivers, police officers, subway riders, restaurant employees, apartment managers, and even some students. These people and many others are getting tired of behaviors that disregard the rights of others. They are often cowered by fear, but they do support us.

Even the courts, in spite of what we hear to the contrary, are helping:

April 25, 1983

U.S.A. PRISON POPULATION HITS PEAK AT 412,303 (U.S.A. Today, April 25, 1983, p. 1)

August 29, 1984

PRISON POPULATION SOARING RECORD 454,136 DOUBLE THAT OF A DECADE AGO
(Chicago Tribune, August 29, 1984, p. 1, sec. 1)

September 15, 1986

NATIONAL PRISON POPULATION RECORD 529,000 SAYS
THE JUSTICE DEPARTMENT
(The Free Press, September 15, 1986, p. 3)

What politician would rather spend money for incarceration than education? What parent wants their child to attend an unruly school? We have a lot of support!

The second step we need to take to help our society become a better place is to remember that in spite of the HEADLINES and the outrageous behavior we hear, we are doing a pretty good job! Yes, certainly cemeteries are vandalized and windows are broken and automobiles are painted; but, when we consider the free time youths have, the availability of spray paint and rocks, perhaps we should be amazed we have as little vandalism as we do. People still cue up for buses, even in downtown Berkeley, and people still share umbrellas on rainy days, even in New York City. And the vast majority of people has as much need to give love as to be loved. Compassionate acts still affect them.

The third step we will need to take to help make our country a better place to live is the hardest. We will have to stop making excuses for the lack of discipline, i.e.: "Look, these people have parents, too; I can't undo years of neglect in one semester." Or, "The state has chosen to empty the mental hospitals onto the streets; what can they expect?." Or, "There are not enough good jobs to go around; why should kids, knowing their best hope is a minimum-wage job, buy into conformity?" There is, of course, some truth in the above statements, but to use them as an excuse compounds the problem.

If we as the educational leaders of our country, the only ones having access to every student, are to make our society a better place for everyone, we will need to remember that we have support, that we are doing a good job (but could do more), and that excuses may make us feel better but don't do much to help.

How do we react to our elderly parents when they forget to respect our rights? How do we react to our own children when they make mistakes? We remind them and show them the correct way. We use kindness and reason. We make the time to help so we don't have to reinvent the wheel every day.

It takes effort to discover why people do what they do, and it takes time to discuss with someone what behavior is in their own best interests; but, if we can remember that discipline is the most important subject we teach and that a lot of people will be affected by how we teach it, perhaps we will make that time.

References

<u>Chicago Tribune</u>. 29 August 1984, sec. 1: 1.

<u>The Free Press</u> [Mankato, Minnesota]. February 1979.

---. 7 May 1983: 10.

---. 9 January 1986.

---. 4 March 1986: 13.

---. 15 September 1986: 3.

<u>Minneapolis Star Tribune</u>. 7 August 1985: 68.

National Institute of Education. <u>Violent Schools, Safe Schools: The Safe School Study Report to Congress</u>. Vol I. Washington, D.C.: NIE, 1978. 168.

<u>USA Today</u>. 25 April 1983: 1.

CHAPTER III

THE EXTENT OF THE PROBLEM

The intent of this chapter is to present what four national reports, two national surveys, three state studies, and four recent newspaper headlines say about the magnitude of our nation's discipline problem. I have tried to make it readable and hope it will assist you in putting your discipline problems into perspective.

What do we know about the extent of discipline problems in our nation's schools? And from what sources does this information come?

The most comprehensive knowledge we have, at the national level, is still the Violent Schools, Safe Schools (National Institute of Education, 1978) study conducted a decade ago. This report, sometimes called the National Institute of Education Study or the N.I.E. Study or Safe School Study, was begun in 1974 and completed in 1977.

As information from this report has been widely disseminated, I'll remind you of only three of its findings: (1) sixty-four percent of the junior high teachers said students swore or made obscene gestures at them during the past month; (2) twelve percent of the teachers said they had hesitated to confront misbehaving students for fear of their own safety at least once during the past month; and (3) approximately two-thirds of the personal thefts and robberies, two-thirds of the assaults requiring medical treatment, and nearly three-fourths of the property damage that occurred in school went unreported to police.

Our second most comprehensive study was also completed over a decade ago. In 1976, the Subcommittee to Investigate Juvenile Delinquency conducted hearings. This committee, chaired by Birch Bayh, talked with hundreds of individuals and made their final report (the Bayh Report) in 1977 (Bayh, 1977).

Their findings generally supported the Safe School Study. They reported: (1) that there is abundant evidence that a significant and growing number of schools in urban, suburban, and rural areas

15

are confronting serious levels of violence and vandalism; (2) that although 13-20-year-olds make up only 9% of the population, they account for 50% of the arrests for property crime and 33% of the arrests for violence; and (3) that over 66% of those robberies and 50% of these assaults occur in our schools.

A third source of information is the National School Boards Association Report called Discipline in Our Big City Schools (National School Boards Association, 1977). This study, a survey of 100 school districts throughout the United States, reported that: (1) there is 3.2 times as much fighting at the junior high level as there is at the senior high; and (2) that 2.2 times as many students in junior high school refuse to obey as do in high school.

In addition to the N.I.E. Study, the Bayh Report, and the NSBA Big City Schools Report, in 1983, the Office of Juvenile Justice and Delinquency Prevention studied seven school districts (Weis, 1983). They learned: (1) that in the district with the lowest crime level, 42.6% of the students had items stolen from them, and 5.5% were victims of physical attack during the past year; and (2) that in the district with the highest rate of self-reported crime, 72.2% had items stolen and 19.5% were physically attacked.

In 1977-78, the National Education Association teacher opinion poll (Weis, 1983) concluded that: (1) 17% of our country's teachers were in constant fear of physical attack; and (2) 12% were, during the 1977-78 school year, threatened with attack. The N.E.A. 1983 opinion poll concluded that (1) 5% of the teachers had been attacked; (2) 25% were concerned with being physically attacked; and (3) 50% believed discipline problems interfered to a moderate or greater degree with their teaching.

In addition to the four national studies and two N.E.A. surveys mentioned, several city and state studies have been conducted. I'll report on three.

The first is from California. In 1981, California released the findings of a five-month study (Baker, March 1985, pp. 482-487). During this five-month period: (1) 24 teachers and 215 students were assaulted each day; (2) 100,000 incidents of violence occurred; and (3) 10 million dollars worth of school property was destroyed.

The second is from Boston. In 1982-83, the Boston Safe Schools Commission conducted two studies (Fox, 1983; Seashore, 1983). They reported that: (1) 80% of the minority students and 60% of the white students felt there was a serious problem with crime and violence in their school; (2) 75% of the teachers in junior high said they were swore at or had an obscene gesture made at them during the previous month; (3) 36% of the teachers said a student had threatened to hurt them during the previous month; and (4) 37% of the male students and 17% of the female students reported that they carried, at least on occasion, weapons to school.

And the third comes from Detroit. In 1983, the Detroit Free Press conducted a survey (Macnow, September 19, 1983, p. 1A). They reported that: (1) 66% of the teachers stated that unmotivated and undisciplined students caused serious problems; (2) 46% of the teachers said they were threatened with violence during the previous year; and (3) 19% reported being hit by a student.

I'll conclude this brief review of the extent of discipline problems in our schools by sharing four headlines. These items are not about schools, but are about those we have or have had in our classrooms.

March 29, 1986

YOUTH GO ON RAMPAGE IN CHIC PALM SPRINGS

Palm Springs, Calif (AP) Youths rampaged through this desert resort Friday, dumping water into open-top cars, ripping clothes from women, publicly exposing themselves, and tossing beer containers at police, witnesses said (The Free Press, March 29, 1986, p. 6).

August 30, 1986

ELABORATE FUNERAL HELD FOR CALIFORNIA
VILLAIN MITCHELL

Oakland, Calif (AP) Friends cheered and snapped pictures Friday as convicted drug kingpin Felix Mitchell was carried in an ornate bronze casket to his funeral in an eight-mile procession

17

of limousines and Rolls Royces (The Free Press, August 30, 1986, p. 1).

September 2, 1986

BEACH MOB TORCHES EMERGENCY VEHICLES

Huntington Beach, Calif (AP) Thousands of people watching a surfing contest went on a rampage after police tried to rescue several women whose bikini tops had been torn off, and 1. people were arrested before order was restored (The Free Press, September 2, 1986, p. 30).

September 16, 1986

MAN BEATEN, ROBBED FOLLOWING COLLISION

Cranston, R.I. (AP) A man's gold tooth was yanked out with pliers during a beating and robbery after he lost control of his car and smashed into another vehicle in a park, police said (The Free Press, September 16, 1989, p. 5).

Please believe that our country needs your judgment, guidance, and stability. It has not rewarded, respected, or appreciated you as it should but, please, do not let these injustices weaken your resolve.

As a member of the most important and influencial profession in the world, you stand between unbridled chaos and a civilized society for everyone. You are needed now more than ever.

References

Baker, Keith. "Research Evidence of a School Discipline Problem." Phi Delta Kappan (March 1985): 482-487.

Bayh, Birch. Challenge for the Third Century: Education in a Safe Environment--Final Report on the Nature and Prevention of School Violence and Vandalism. Washington, D.C.: U.S. Government Printing Office, 1977.

Fox, James S. Violence, Victimization, and Discipline in Four Boston Public High Schools. Boston: Safe Schools Commission, 1983.

The Free Press [Mankato, Minnesota]. 29 March 1986: 6.

---. 30 August 1986: 1.

---. 2 September 1986: 30.

---. 16 September 1986: 6.

Macnow, Glen. "Violence Casts Pall over Teachers' Lives." Detroit Free Press, 19 September 1983: 1A.

National Education Association. Teacher Opinion Poll. Washington, D.C.: N.E.A., 1978.

National Institute of Education. Violent Schools, Safe Schools: The Safe School Study Report to the Congress. Vol 1. Washington, D.C.: N.I.E., 1978.

National School Boards Association. Report: Discipline in Our Big City Schools. Washington, D.C.: National School Boards Association, 1977.

Seashore, Karen S. Boston Teachers' Views about Problems of Violence and Discipline in the Public Schools. Boston: Safe Schools Commission, 1983.

Weis, J. Evaluation of Delinquency Prevention Research and Development Project. Seattle: Center for Law and Justice, University of Washington, 1983.

CHAPTER IV

WHY STUDENTS MISBEHAVE

Students misbehave. No one disputes this. Eighty to 90% have committed crimes for which they could be arrested (Hawkins & Doueck, 1984); each year, 1,500,000 are arrested (Regnery, Fall 1985); and since the Depression area, juvenile arrests have increased 9,300% (Office of Juvenile Justice and Delinquency Prevention, 1984).

Students shatter mirrors, destroy towel dispensers, felt-tip entire walls. Would knowing why matter? Or, do students simply act as they do because adults lack the guts to make them mind?

Years ago, I worked with student teachers at a state hospital. Many of their students were mentally handicapped adults, and most either screamed, messed their pants, drooled, pulled hair, or openly masturbated. Would hysteria and commands and demands have improved their behavior? No, because they could not choose to behave better. They were behaving, at least at that moment, in the only way they knew how.

My point? If our goal is to react to discipline problems in ways that prevent such behaviors in the future and encourage students to act like ladies and gentlemen when we are not around--then knowing if a child can behave; knows appropriate ways to behave; and is aware she is misbehaving--may be vital base knowledge.

Attitudes toward such questions matter, because how we perceive problems determines how we react, and how we handle discipline problems now will determine the kind of society we will all share in the future. When we react to discipline problems, we are always modeling how others might one day handle similar problems.

A mediator can't settle every dispute; an arbitrator can't handle every grievance; a police person can't be on every corner. Our country needs citizens who can and will conduct themselves properly when authority figures are not around.

That is a tall order, I know, but we have 165 to 180 days a year and 12 or 13 years to teach this.

Every day we can model ways to handle people who are rude; every day we can prompt self-affection; and every day we can assist students in understanding the needs behind behavior.

If our goal is to react to discipline problems in ways that stop the behavior now and prevent it in the future, then our knowledge of: (1) <u>can a child behave</u>; (2) <u>does a child know how to behave</u>; and (3) <u>does a child know he is misbehaving</u>, becomes important.

It is hard to keep from taking student insults personally; it is difficult not to engage in knee-jerk reactions; and it's often impossible to cool down before reacting. But, if we could, our society would be better off.

Students don't always bug us deliberately. They don't hurt us because they want to. They want us to like them. We don't believe these truths, I know. But, it is not because they aren't true--it's rather because we haven't stopped to make the time to examine why kids misbehave. So, here goes.

There are hundreds of reasons why students misbehave, such as: their levels of hormones are too high; they see society as deserving criticism and reshaping; they do not have enough intelligence to learn from experience; religion is not an integral part of their lives (Stark, October 1979); or because their parents' incomes are very high (Meyers & Maine, March 1, 1985). We could go on--gangs, racism, poverty, child abuse.

When I ask educators why students misbehave, they say it is because students want attention; see too much violence on television; have low self-concepts; have no supervision at home; are bored; don't know any better; eat too much refined sugar; and because they are exposed to wishy-washy inconsistent administrators.

When I ask myself why kids misbehave, I say 80% do for one or more of these eight reasons. The first is letter grades. Over half of our secondary students are harmed by them. Over half of our students are made to feel like perpetual losers by them (Glasser, 1969, p. 149). If caring, cooperation, and fairness were rewarded as we now reward abstract reasoning, memory, and the ability to deal with verbal and mathematical abstractions, we would see better behaved students. Any group that believes they are controlled by a person who does not value <u>their</u> knowledge, is unconcerned about what <u>they</u> think, and is oblivious to <u>their</u> feelings, cannot be expected to conform. Would you conform if your boss didn't care one hoot about you?

Secondly, students misbehave because of poor eyesight, lack of sleep, hearing problems, and hunger. Do you remember going without your glasses for a day or sitting for an hour when you couldn't hear the speaker? Most unmet needs keep us from being civil. Parents care. Could we seek their help? Sometimes big problems <u>do</u> have simple solutions and sometimes we do overlook the obvious.

Third, an irrelevant curriculum. Forty percent of today's seniors enter the workforce upon graduation and 70% work while in school (Smart, October 19, 1986, p. 1F; Wisconsin Center for Educational Research News, Summer 1984, pp. 5-6). Do we tap this as we should? Do we relate course work to jobs?

Fourth, many students see the future as looking hopeless; they do not see the future bringing something better. We need to help these students understand that they are the creators of their own happiness, that freedom comes with self-discipline, and that they have a most precious gift--freedom of choice. They need to know that good wins over evil! Yes, con artists, hustlers, liars, thieves, and cheaters do win in the short haul, but not in the long run. Employers don't hire cheats. They hire those with integrity and honesty. Those who sell their souls for temporary gain eventually lose. Some mysterious force seems to level the bumps. Students need to know this. And they need to know that there are still people who value those who stand up for what is right, what is decent, even if it is unpopular with co-workers and acquaintances.

Fifth, students misbehave because parents have changed. Books such as Benjamin Fine's <u>1,000,000 Delinquents</u> written in 1955, Walter Smith's 1924 book <u>Constructive School Discipline</u>; Emerson White's <u>School Management</u>; and Horace Mann's <u>Fourth Report</u> written in 1840, make it clear that children yesterday and today are quite alike. Yesterday, students needed to learn, needed approval, needed to test authority, and needed to be liked; they also desired to grow up instantly, wanted to belong, and had fears. The changing variable? Parents. We may not like it and may feel it unfair, but, for some children, we <u>are</u> the "parent." We <u>are</u> the only ones they can trust enough to talk to--the only ones with whom they will ever share what they so desperately need to say.

Sixth, students misbehave because they are trapped by their reputations. They want out, but do not see a way. If we could look beyond their upside-down, backward, and smart talk, we might see a person quite willing to change.

Seventh, educators have been too timid in reading the U.S. Supreme Court rulings. The Supreme Court wants us to maintain a suitable learning environment (Stern, 1984), and they are quite aware that "without first establishing discipline and maintaining order, teachers cannot begin to educate their students" (Mahoney, Spring 1985, p. 29). The Supreme Court has not abolished corporal punishment. Students can still be suspended and expelled. Lockers and students can still be searched (Carrington, Winter 1985, pp. 16-17). The United States Supreme Court has bent over backwards <u>not</u> to tie our hands. (This issue will be discussed in more detail in Chapter XIII.)

And, finally, children misbehave because too much emphasis has been placed on what is best for the child and too little on what is best for society.

In conclusion, let me suggest that before we react to misbehavior, we remember the following: (1) that there are scores of reasons why students misbehave; (2) that when we discipline, we are modeling how students themselves might solve problems in the future; and (3) that knowing why a student misbehaves may help us present a solution that will help children behave now and when we are no longer there to guide them.

References

Carrington, Frank. "Student Searches: Still Looking for Answers." _School Safety_ (Winter 1985): 16-17.

Fine, Benjamin. _1,000,000 Delinquents_. Cleveland and New York: The World Publishing Company, 1955.

Glasser, William. _Schools without Failure_. New York: Harper and Row, 1969. 149.

Hawkins, David, Jr., and Howard Doueck. _Social Development and the Prevention of Antisocial Behavior among Low Achievers_. Seattle: National Center for the Assessment of Delinquent Behavior and its Prevention, School of Social Work, University of Washington, 1984.

Mahoney, Diane. "Legal Update: New Jersey v. T.L.O.--The Lay of the Law." _School Safety_ (Spring 1985): 29.

Mann, Horace. _Fourth Annual Report: Covering the Year 1840_. Boston: Dullon and Wentworth, 1841.

Meyers, David, and Ann Maine. A study for the U.S. Office of Education and in a paper presented on March 1, 1985, to the American Educational Research Association in Chicago.

Office of Juvenile Justice and Delinquency Prevention. Washington, D.C.: _Report of the N.I.J.J.D.P. Fiscal Years 1983-1984_, 1984.

Regnery, Alfred S. "Getting Away with Murder--Why the Juvenile Justice System Needs an Overhaul." _Policy Review_ 34 (Fall 1985).

Smart, William E. "Opinions Split on Job's Value to a Student." _Minneapolis Star Tribune_, 19 October 1986: 1F.

Smith, Walter R. _Constructive School Discipline_. New York: American Book Company, 1924.

References

Stark, Rodney. <u>Religion and Delinquency: The Ecology of a "Lost" Relationship</u>. Seattle: National Institute for Juvenile Justice and Delinquency Prevention Center for Law and Justice, University of Washington, October 1979.

Stern, Ralph D. <u>Interface: Schools and the Law</u>. Austin: National Alliance for Safe Schools, 1984.

White, Emerson E. <u>School Management</u>. New York: American Book Company, 1893.

Wisconsin Center for Educational Research News. "Student Jobs Affect Teaching and Learning." Summer 1984: 5-6.

CHAPTER V

DISCIPLINE AND THE FIRST-YEAR TEACHER

What do teachers learn about discipline in their first year of teaching that isn't taught in college? For years I've asked this question. And, surprisingly, at least to me, I have always received a ready answer. Veteran teachers remember vividly their problems in that first year of teaching. What follows are 10 of their comments, my reactions, and three short bits of advice.

Comment #1

"You are now entering the 'real' world. You will find that after spending four years in college studying this vocation, you are unprepared. The first year will be your real education, the kids your toughest instructors. You will find yourself on your own; few will support you or tell you what a nice job you are doing. Administrators are to be looked upon with suspicion; at times, they will back you, but, more frequently, they will cut you. It's tough, but, it's the best education you'll ever get.

"Good luck! You'll need it!"

Reaction: Since you will have no frame of reference and no stockpile of experience to draw upon, you'll make mistakes. Expect to--but also try to learn from them. Every mistake you make and learn from now will be one less you will make as a veteran.

Comment #2

"The first thing I learned is that students are going to test you because you are new. And then they are going to retest you to see if you can hang in there. You have to be stronger than they are . . . ."

Reaction: Welcome student criticism. If you can get a group that is open and will level with you, rejoice--they'll make a teacher out of you.

Don't be overly concerned about being conned. It doesn't take long to separate the serious from those setting you up. Besides, if you're being made too big a fool, your students will rat on each other. That's one of the real joys of teaching--seeing students' fair play in action. Their sense of fair play far exceeds that of most adults.

Comment #3

"Being a first-year teacher is difficult, stressful, and a whole lot more work than any you ever imagined."

Reaction: A similar comment was made by nearly all of my graduate students.

Comment #4

"Try to second guess what might occur and how you would handle it so you don't do something off the wall."

Reaction: Like keeping the entire class in because someone emptied the pencil sharpener in a corner of the room. Sometimes no one confesses, because no one in that class did it.

Comment #5

"You will have behavior problems--the best do."

Reaction: As a graduate student, I recall a professor telling us how the drop-out rate for inner-city student teachers changed from 80% incompletes to 80% completing the semester. This was accomplished by using role playing. A student, about to student teach, was asked to teach three adults for half an hour. These adults played the roles of students--they were rude, crude, disruptive, abusive, and disrespectful. Sometimes the student teachers cried and fled the room, but they were always calmed down, talked to, given advice, and urged to continue.

Anticipating is the first step many veterans urge, because when you expect something, you are not caught off guard, and you are more apt to behave with sound judgment.

Comment #6

"Don't be a jerk in the lounge. Teaching is complicated. Don't start off by offending those who can help."

Reaction: I often wonder how a new teacher, challenged by a multitude of decisions, with a minimum of time to consider alternatives, and having no experience to call upon, gets the courage even to try. Nothing will be more important for you than to find one person you respect and trust to confide in during that first year. Principals often assign mentors to first-year teachers. If one isn't assigned to you, ask for one, or find a buddy among the more experienced teachers.

Comment #7

"Disciplining students will take up much of your time. I made extensive lesson plans, but discipline took up so much of my time, I never got through them."

Reaction: True, a well-planned lesson doesn't stop all discipline problems. But, a disorganized, unprepared teacher, instead of having problems, has chaos. Believe that what you are teaching is important, that it is necessary for your students to learn it, and that class time is too important to be wasted. Parents of your well-behaved students have rights, too. They do not want you to let immature, short-sighted, disruptive students cheat their child out of an education.

Comment #8

"Don't be a yeller and a screamer. They will just tune you out."

Reaction: This, of course, is true. But, beyond that, yelling and screaming can be harmful. Yelling and screaming provide therapy for the teacher and amusement for the cut-ups, but it often terrorizes the quiet and timid. Quiet students are your greatest allies. If push comes to shove, and it becomes secret ballot time, they will be on your side. Don't alienate them. Their needs are as great as your troublemakers' needs. They just don't wear them on their sleeves. Teach the quiet ones how to become more asserive. And teach them by example ways they themselves might react to similar problems such as late parties at public campgrounds, swearing on public buses, and loud talking in movie theaters. It isn't written in stone that bullies and con artists will inherit the earth.

29

Comment #9

"If it's necessary for you to be labeled a tyrant--then let it be. Many first-year teachers want to be popular and become 'buddies' with students. I feel it is more important to be respected at first."

Reaction: Also learn to say no. Ignore the hurt looks and why-nots, and just say no. It is much easier to change a no to yes than vice versa. Being called Mr. and Ms., having others ask you for permission, being respected--this is pretty heavy stuff. But what is so easily given can be easily taken away. Student cliques can make or break a teacher. The popular ones, the leaders, the "in" groups can laugh at the misfit and make you laugh along, because if you don't, they can bring out their deadly stares, their cold shoulders, their vicious rumors, and the game playing that will quickly let you know who is really boss. It takes courage to stand up for those too weak to defend themselves; it takes courage to forego popularity to do the right and decent thing; and it takes courage to buck the system and to stop giving those who need the least help the most.

Train yourself to rely on sources other than popularity for a sense of well-being. Derive satisfaction from seeing students learn, from the quiet becoming more outspoken, and from the self-centered learning to care about others.

Comment #10

"I have watched new teachers in our department go through some pretty hard first years. My suggestion to them would be to use the 'assertive discipline' approach."

Reaction: Lee Canter's approach of writing a student's name on the board and making a check mark behind it if she misbehaves works, because it spells out what a teacher will not tolerate, and because it encourages even the most timid teacher to act. Have high expectations. Be aware, however, that assertive discipline does little to change attitudes. Our checking their names, making them stay after school, and rewarding their "good" behavior keeps them in check while in our rooms, but does little to make them behave when we are not around.

Be suspicious of any quick fix. Try to find out what is behind behavior. Before you act quickly, ask yourself these three questions:

--Can a child I'm about to yell at behave?

--Does she know the correct way to behave?

--Is she aware she is misbehaving?

Sometimes discipline is as simple as teaching the correct ways to behave, reminding students that they are out of line, and accepting what cannot be changed. We can always resort to punishment. Why not try understanding and reason first?

In closing, three bits of advice:

1. When it comes to discipline, remember, there are no easy solutions and no persons, even seasoned veterans, with all the answers. Teaching is the most complicated job in the world! Not everyone can teach at the elementary or secondary level. And the main reason they cannot is that "little" thing called discipline.

Just do your best and don't allow your first group to be selfish beasts. You may teach for 40 years. Don't let one group, your first, drive you out. In five years you may be the best teacher alive. Don't allow one group to rob the thousands you may one day help!

2. Resolve before you start, (a) that you don't deserve to be trampled upon; (b) that you have something to offer others; and (c) that you are a human being and deserve a fair chance.

3. Before your first day, remind yourself of the characteristics of a good boss--a person you'll walk across the street to introduce to your parents. Does she respect you, listen to you, treat you as if you have a brain? Is she friendly toward you, accepting, caring, genuine, and fair?

Remember, you are your students' boss. What you like and admire in others they will like and admire in you.

CHAPTER VI

DISCIPLINE AND WHAT YOU MIGHT SHARE WITH PARENTS

Parents determine the quality of life we all experience. If our neighbors and co-workers are pleasant, parents merit most of the credit. If they are not, parents deserve much of the blame. Parents have a most important job, one that affects everyone.

Parenthood is also a job that offers much--opportunities for personal growth, occasions for feeling significant, and moments of deep satisfaction.

Of course, many parents do not see their job this way. Many do not feel that being a parent is important, do not believe their behavior impacts others, and do not experience joy or satisfaction from the job. For these parents, parenthood is something to be endured.

I understand these feelings, but, nonetheless, they unsettle me. For, like you, I have to live by, live with, and work beside these unhappy parents and, in time, we'll have to live by, and work beside, their disgruntled children.

I believe, however, there is hope. I believe the job of being a parent can be put into a more manageable perspective.

Parenthood doesn't have to be a continuous shouting match--a sentence to be served; it can be a rewarding experience, as well. And parents can begin to live what is life now, years before the last child leaves the nest.

For these changes to occur, at least three things are necessary. First, parents will need to accept at least four of the realities that surround parenthood. Second, parents will need to decide what they expect from their children. And, third, parents will need to learn what they can believe about children.

The first reality surrounding parenthood is that parents are wiser than they think they are. We are all blessed with built-in guidance systems. If we go too far--spank too aggressively or yell and scream without being in control--we feel guilt. If we ignore acts we know we should not--selfish, inconsiderate, irresponsible behavior--we feel anxiety, uneasiness, and frustration. Parents need to more frequently recognize and then act upon these persistent feelings. The system is in place--we just need to listen to it.

The second reality is that much of the expert advice we hear only clouds the water.

One groups says: Look, if you spank your child, he will grow up and hit his own children; he will resolve all of his conflicts through violence. Fear will only cause him to repress his anger while you are around, but it will surface later--he will be a rapist, a sniper, or a hit man.

Then the other group says: Wait a minute. Look, if you let your child make choices, be free, do what she wants, she will grow up to be a selfish, spoiled brat--inconsiderate of everyone but herself. That is what's wrong with our society. Kids think the world owes them a living. They desire a million dollar lifestyle with a three dollar skill level. They drink when they want, swear when they want, play their loud music when they want--they even work when they want. What kids need today is some good old-fashioned discipline.

Both arguments have merit--what's a parent to believe?

First, believe that not all purveyors of "advice" know what they are talking about. Some have allowed time to crowd out reality, some haven't raised children, and some need to get their act together before continuing to advise anyone. Have reservations about what's being presented you--this chapter included.

Second, believe that you are not alone; others are also having difficulties sorting out this barrage of conflicting information.

And, third, believe, or perhaps just realize, that those who present information via way of television, radio, a book, or an article, do not even know your child. Trust yourself--trust your judgment--trust your guidance system.

The third reality is that when it comes to day-to-day discipline, you are alone. Don't expect support.   Instead, expect to hear,   "Everyone else is going--why am I the only one who can't?"

You have bedtimes for your children. Do your neighbors?   You don't let your children ride their bicycles in the street.   Do other parents have the same rules?   Unless you live in a neighborhood where parents share similar values, you are alone.   But, remember, you are wiser than you think you are and you know your children better than anyone. Don't be afraid of the word <u>no</u> or the flak that will follow; and don't allow yourself to be intimidated by those whose standards are more lax than your own. Parenthood is the most important occupation in the world--why wouldn't it demand great courage?

The fourth and last reality is that <u>there are no guarantees attached to parenthood</u>.   You can do your best, hope for the best, but still fall short.   Some parents are way underpowered and fall short often, but many good parents do likewise. They, through no fault of their own, seem to be besieged with problems, such as children becoming a parent unexpectedly, children being incarcerated, children being involved in drugs, children hurting or killing someone in an accident.

What's a parent to do--throw up their hands and give up? No, of course not. Do your best to raise children who can satisfy their needs without harming themselves or others, but, at the same time, recognize that your best shot may not always hit your mark.   The fear of failure is a burden every parent carries--a burden <u>every</u> parent carries. All you can expect from yourself and all that society can expect is that you do the best with what that creative force behind our universe has chosen to give.

Once these realities have been acknowledged: (1) that you are wiser than you think you are; (2) that even though you are surrounded by experts, you still have to trust your own judgment; (3) that when it comes to day-to-day discipline, you are alone; and (4) that there are no guarantees attached to parenthood, the next step toward making parenthood more rewarding is to decide what goals and expectations you have for your children.

Goals are important because they serve as guides. They help us decide whether an action is appropriate. Goals other parents have endorsed are: raising children who would avoid crack or similar drugs and raising children who would not need to turn to a gang for personal protection, acceptance, status, and self-worth. Your list, undoubtedly, will be longer and perhaps more specific.

So, think through what you expect. If you know what long-term outcomes you are striving for, even if they are just things you don't want your children to do, your patterns of behavior will take on direction. You will have reasons for why you act (remember, however, that inaction is action).

Once you have decided upon your expectations, the last step toward becoming a more satisfied parent is to learn what can be believed about children.

First, you can safely believe that children are flexible. Children can behave one way in one classroom and be another person in the next. They can behave one way toward one parent and behave completely different toward the other. They can fight with a "friend" one minute and want to play with him or her the next.

Consequently, you should not feel undue guilt when you do not meet all of their needs when they want them met. Nothing is wrong with saying, "I just got off work, Marc; I'll talk to you in just a bit. Let me rest and call me when 20 minutes are up." Children can handle this--they may not like it--but they are flexible enough to handle it. If your needs are not always relegated to second place, the attention you do give will have a higher likelihood of being more genuine.

Second, you can believe that children read non-verbal behavior far more accurately than they do verbal behavior.

Third, you can safety believe that children want to be good rather than bad. Children are social creatures and know their needs are more genuinely met when they are good. It is important that parents understand this concept, for, more often than not, when children bug us, it's because they have not yet learned a more appropriate way to get attention. When given a choice and some direction, children will behave positively rather than negatively.

Fourth, you can believe that children like boundaries. They find security in knowing what to expect. Your rules not only provide this security, they also protect your child from his or her own inexperience and ignorance.

Fifth, you can safely believe that if children have a say in the rules, most will religiously adhere to them. Chldren have a sense of fair play unequaled by most adults. Ninety-nine percent of the enforcement problem disappears. They will even take it upon themselves` to scold violators. What they understand, they learn and accept.

Sixth, children who live by railroad tracks in time do not hear the trains. Parents need to understand that rantings and ravings, though often therapeutic for the parent, are eventually ignored.

And, last, you can safely believe that children can handle temporary setbacks if their feelings have been understood, if they have been given a choice, or if they have been able to have their say. To clarify, let me use this example: The bus was due one minute ago, it is raining, and your child refuses to wear her raincoat. In solving this problem, one approach might be: "I understand that others don't wear raincoats and you feel yours is ugly. I understand that you feel I'm just trying to embarrass you, but you will either wear your raincoat or when you get home, go directly to your room and stay there all evening. I'll bring your supper to you." (Not much of a choice, but a choice, nonetheless.) Or, you might say, "I cannot afford any doctor bills this month, and you will wear your raincoat today. Tonight we'll talk about it, and perhaps this payday we can get you a coat we both like." (Here the feelings have been accepted and the child knows he'll get his say.)

We could spend pages dealing with specific behavior problems such as stealing, lying, tattling, selfishness, not doing homework, excessive meanness, etc.--things all parents encounter. But, who am I to start giving you specific suggestions about how to raise your child. If you have accepted some of the realities of parenthood, if you have established in your own mind what kind of an adult you would like your child to become, and if you have begun to better understand that children want boundaries, want to be good, and accept what they understand, etc., you have already progressed beyond my abilities to help.

CHAPTER VII

A PERSPECTIVE ON DISCIPLINE

Most of us have been concerned about discipline at least from the time of our first pre-student teaching clinical experiences. In addition, most of us have spent more time thinking about and discussing this topic than we realize. Seldom, however, do we spend time searching for a consistent viewpoint about discipline which could guide our behavior.

During the past 10 years, hundreds of articles dealing with discipline have appeared in major professional journals. Numbers of books and task force publications have dealt with the same topic. I have discovered, however, that the more seriously and systematically I've approached this topic, the more inadquate I feel. Nonetheless, in spite of these feelings, I have come to believe some things about discipline, and I do have some insights I'd like to share.

First of all, in terms of teaching--and this is true regardless of one's philosophy--I think one has to believe that schooling is vital to the United States. Without schools, our society would be in a state of utter confusion. In addition to this belief about schooling, teachers need to believe that what they are teaching is essential to the survival, happiness, and enjoyment of students in their later lives. I believe teachers have to decide right away-- regardless of what they are teaching--that the material they are covering is important for their students' happiness and perhaps even for their survival. If your curriculum is such that you can't say that, I think you have to revamp it, because I don't see how a techer could really sell himself and be enthusiastic unless he believes what he is teaching is important.

The second thing I have come to believe is that you, as a teacher, will have to do your best to be a person your students can respect, and you will have to do your best to teach in a way that makes the material palatable. If you were a student sitting in your own classroom, would what is going on be palatable to you? However, it's also important that students be made aware that all learning can't be fun and games; it can't all be like television. It can't end neatly in

30 minutes with a nice epilogue. If you do try to be
the same type of person that kids can respect, do
teach so that the material has relevance, and if you
do make them understand that school can't be all
games, you have a big edge. That's also when you can
say, during the beginning portion of class, "All
right, what's going on? I've really been trying. We
have varied activities. We have been in groups.
We've tried to allow all of you to be involved--and
you guys are just not cooperating. What's wrong?" In
this instance, of course, you're appealing to their
sense of fair play; and because they know that you
have been trying, they will, at least, share some of
the responsibility for what has gone wrong. But, if
you haven't been trying to make the class interesting
and if you drone on, then you might as well forget
leveling with the class as a technique, because I
think that it will fail. If you have tried, however,
leveling is one advantage you'll always have, for
students have a keen sense of fair play.

The third item I've come to believe is that a
teacher has to believe that kids have a natural desire
to learn and that this desire is as natural as eating,
drinking, and going to the bathroom. Kids, as well as
you and I, have a need to learn and a need to grow.
Just recall any time you have been depressed or
unhappy. Most often it was because you were not
planning anything; you were not looking forward to
anything. You were not reading anything or examining
anything that would allow you to grow and expand
yourself. You were not allowing you to become bigger
than yourself. Some of you might say, "Now, wait a
minute. I've got a class that nothing will motivate.
Nothing I try motivates them." That's because this
need is just latent, and you have got to get it up to
the surface. It has been beaten down, but it is still
there. I think you have to believe it's still there;
it's just got to be drawn to the surface.

The fourth insight I'd like to share is that you
might--on occasion--have to take this attitude: "If
you are going to goof around in school, why don't you
save your parents' money and hang out at the local
Phillips 66 station, because no one has the right to
interfere with anyone else's right to learn. My
responsibility is to the taxpayers and the parents of
the other kids in this classroom, too." Of course, if
they would take you up on this offer and leave for
downtown, you would have a big problem. Most, of

40

course, would not; but if they would, it's time for in-school suspension. Students must be made to understand that their parents pay thousands of dollars in taxes each year for their "free" education.

Sometimes it pays to allow kids to see the extremes of a continuum. In one instance, my own sons were yelling and hitting each other. I said, "All right, if you want to hit and hurt each other, I'll take you down to Spring Lake Park and you can each get 10 of the biggest rocks you can find. I want you to take turns throwing rocks at each other. You can't cover up your face; you just have to stand there." They got very quiet. It shook them up. For perhaps the first time, they were able to see fighting in a different perspective. I think on occasion you may need to allow your students to see the extreme.

The fifth item I'd like to share is that it is critical to match discipline with the student and with the incident. That's why it's very hard to make a flat statement such as, "Spanking is wrong." I don't think I would ever spank a child, and I don't think I would ever hit a child. I think it would be better to handle his/her and my problem in some other way. But, I can also see that there may be times when a spanking would possibly be quite appropriate--for example, with the boy who always puts gravy and mashed potatoes in the retarded girl's hair. If individual conferences with his parents have failed, and quiet-room time has failed, and if talks with the psychologist have indicated that he's just a healthy boy, then a spanking may be justified.

Generally speaking, those who handle discipline problems by talking alone with students do a better job of not only matching the discipline with the students, but also are less likely to be guilty of unsettling the many for the wrongdoing of the few. I firmly believe that unless someone has killed another human being, everything regarding disruptive behavior can be handled by allowing the student to see himself as others see him. This, of course, is not easy. It requires careful observation skills on the teacher's part.

For example, when dealing with a student with a problem, I've done the following. I've had a student come in, sit down, put the books away, and just sit for a few minutes. Then I've gone over and sat right

41

next to him and have asked: "Did you see anything that you did today which may have been out of line?" Student: "No." "Don, you came to class late, right?" Don: "Yes." "You hit Jim, Joan, and Kevin before you ever sat down, right?" Don: "No, not Kevin; he hit me in P.E. and I was just paying him back." "But you did hit Jim and Joan?" Don: "Yes." "Now, by half-way through the period, by about 10:15, you had sharpened your pencil four times. You made smart remarks about three of the questions I asked, right?" Don: (silence). "You are a good kid, I know that, and like everyone, _even me_, you need to be liked." Don: "I don't care if anyone likes me--I do my thing." "Don, when the coach said 'great' after your tackle last night, I saw you smile. So, let's cut the bull. I want you to be the kind of kid people like and like to be around." (Etc.--for another half-hour)

Generally, kids behave differently after a talk with a teacher, especially if the student knows that the teacher cares and sees that the teacher can present an accurate picture--a picture with at least enough clarity to allow the student to replay it in their own mind. So, in terms of matching discipline with the student and with the incident, it's important to get to know the student well enough so that you can care. It's important for you to find at least one thing to like about them. We are not doing kids any favor by letting them behave in such a way that they alienate everyone--including us.

The sixth item I'd like to share concerns rules. I would suggest setting very few. Three that I've used with success are:

1. "I'll respect your right to speak when you are speaking, and I expect you to respect my right to speak when I'm speaking."

2. "If I'm wrong, I'll apologize."

3. "If I tell you to do something, don't argue with me. Just do it, and if I'm wrong, I'll apologize."

Other teachers make them even simpler. One teacher tells her class, "I'm going to write the rules for the class on the board, and I want you to memorize them." Then she writes, "Show you care about other people." Some teachers I know will let the first weeks of class become total confusion and then let the class develop rules that will improve the situation. The most important consideration about rules is not whether they are imposed or whether they evolve, but rather whether students fully understand why they exist and agree that they are important.

The seventh idea: As teachers, we have the responsibility for developing an environment where everyone can live free of fear. We all know how at times some kids can be very cruel, and we are all aware of the tremendous peer pressue that exists. But, for at least the time during which our students are in our class, we have a responsibility to protect them from anybody who is going to harass them. Here again, this requires us to take risks and to be observant. When I was teaching in a junior high school, I had a student who would sit in the back of the room and snap a girl's bra. She didn't want to say anything because he was a football star, and he was in enough trouble all the time anyway. We have a responsibility to take care of situations such as this, especially when students feel that they can't speak out themselves. When they can't or won't, we have to speak for them and, hopefully, do it in such a way that after-school retaliation will not occur.

The eighth and last item I'd like to share concerns parents. I think it's important that you let students know that you'll talk to their mothers, fathers, or guardians. What is interesting about the parent-versus-teacher topic is that often teachers will say, "Parents don't care. They call the school and complain, and they believe what their sons and daughters tell them." First of all, I don't believe this. I believe that parents are very concerned and that those parents who appear to be concerned the least are actually concerned the most. I believe this because every parent is aware that if education doesn't help their child, nothing is likely to help them. If a problem of non-concern, or its opposite, threats to the school, emerges, it's a problem of how to communicate needs, not a problem of their non-existence.

But let's assume for the moment that it is true--that parents of children who seem to alienate everyone don't care about their sons and daughters. Does it hold that a student will behave more positively if he knows you will call his parents? I believe it does.

Studies in conscience development completed at Stanford University by Sears suggest that children, as early as four or five, have ideas about "appropriate parent" behavior. For example, boys who had never been spanked acted out roles in which they misbehaved. Then they were asked what their mothers would do about their misbehavior. Frequently, they said, "Give me a spanking." Even if parents don't give a damn, <u>kids know they should</u>. In my experience as a teacher and through talks with hundreds of teachers, I've yet to learn about a kid who, when engaging in straight talk, did not get a little uptight about the possibility of a teacher-parent dialogue.

In dealing with behavior problems, it doesn't always take two years to fill in the hole that the student has been digging for two years. Sometimes it just takes a person like you who can make the student believe you do care. I once had a student who was a terror. One day he missed the bus, so I took him home. His mother was there, and we talked for all of 30 seconds. From that day on, he was a completely different kid. In another case, I let a child help me spray for wasps in our classroom. After that afternoon, he was a completely different child. In still another case, I discovered a mean, potential drop-out couldn't hear, not one word. Once his teachers were informed, his behavior not only did a flip-flop, but he also graduated. These are not cases out of an educational psychology textbook--they <u>actually</u> happened!

Our students want to be liked and to have other's approval. It's our job to do what we can to sell education, to sell ourselves, to sell our subject matter, to be sensitive to the fact that students need to learn, to protect those who are at this time too weak to protect themselves, and to help our students see that freedom comes only with some restrictions on freedom. Finally, we must work with anyone who will help us better understand and, consequently, like at least something about every child whom we teach.

CHAPTER VIII

TEN PRINCIPLES FOR WORKING WITH ADOLESCENTS

What follows are excerpts from a paper I wrote 25 years ago. Then it was called <u>A Book of Thirty-Three Psychological Principles</u>. I hope you will find this information as useful today as I did that first summer after my beginning year of teaching.

Principle #1

Teachers should help adolescents understand that to be considered a friend is one of life's most meaningful honors. In answering, "Yes, but how will I know?," you might simply suggest friends are those who can tolerate periods of silence when in each other's company.

Principle #2

We should help adolescents realize their ability to deal with others need not be static. We should assure them that they can make themselves more interesting. One suggestion we might offer--smile more.

To illustrate the effect of a genuine smile, we might share the following: One day the chairman of the psychology department at a major university realized that he was meeting a great number of grumpy people. Since this depressed him and he didn't like to feel depressed, he decided to try something really different. He started giving everyone he saw an honest-to-goodness, sincere smile. He did that for several days. His concluding remarks regarding the experiment were, "I never realized there were so many friendly people on this campus."

Principle #3

Students, especially those entering adolescence, become increasingly conscious of the differences between their parents and other parents. Some become ashamed of their parents. The school should meet this problem head-on and explain that many people of their age feel ashamed of their parents; but as they grow older, they will begin to realize how wonderful their parents are and how really fortunate they are to have them. Perhaps this entire parent-adolescent struggle

45

can be introduced by asking them what they think Mark
Twain meant when he wrote: "When I was a boy of 14,
my father was so stupid that I could scarcely stand to
have the old man around; but, by the time I got to be
21, I was astonished at how much he had learned in the
last seven years."

Principle #4

It is easy to talk of understanding youth. It is
even easy to plan what we will say and how we will
react to what they say in return. But often our
dreams of helping adolescents die on the planning
board. Many times we do not carry through because we
are unable to completely depart from the idea that,
"If they really wanted to be different, to be better,
they could." Teachers may be helped to see this
situation in a more realistic light by considering the
following: Taking into account the social pressures
acting upon adolescents, the experiences they have
had, and the parents they have, most adolescents
behave in about the only way they are capable of
behaving.

Principle #5

Just as anger often results in guilt, so does
fear. For some reason, our culture has developed
cowardice into a synonym for fear. Nothing, of
course, could be farther from the truth. Fear is
simply a normal reaction to a threatening situation.
Our students should be helped to realize this.

Principle #6

Teachers need to be aware that students who
appear to be seriously disturbed comprise only a small
portion of those with unsolved problems. Many times
their problems exist because they are not mature
enough to see that their fears are out of proportion.
As teachers, we must first become sensitive to the
fact that <u>most</u> students have many problems, and then
we must help them see these problems in their proper
perspective.

Principle #7

Too often teachers fail to truly understand the
deep humiliation that follows failure. Failure does
not become less painful just because it is repeated

again and again. To subject many of our students to
daily failure or threat of failure is brutal. A major
objective of the school should be to provide all
students with opportunities to become successful.

Principle #8

In their search for better self-understanding,
students should be reminded often that self-knowledge
is the most difficult knowledge to acquire. If they
could understand this, they might not become so easily
discouraged by all the self-doubts, all the mood
fluctuations, and all the inner confusions that
confront them.

Principle #9

Adolescents need to understand that during this
period of their lives, they will see great physical
changes take place in their body and in those of their
classmates; they need to be assured that girls won't
always be taller than boys, that pimples will
disappear, and that soon boys' voices will stabilize.
Adolescents need to know that they are facing the most
difficult, yet most important, period of their
formative lives. But, they also need to be assured
that one day they will emerge from this period a
mature person, one able and ready to face life's
demands and rewards.

Principle #10

It seems appropriate to close with a message
about the end product of adolescence--maturity.
Maturity is a state that can never be completely
achieved, but nevertheless can have tremendous value
when used as a guiding star. Perhaps the easiest way
to help young people grow in maturity as they grow in
age is to present them with a picture of a mature
person.

A mature person does not say that everything is
either white or black or right or wrong, but rather
sees both sides of an issue.

A mature person is able to put off self-
gratification for future gains and does not live <u>just</u>
for the moment.

A mature person places little value upon

appearances or first impressions.

A mature person is able to control self-pity and realizes that others have problems and griefs as serious as theirs.

A mature person can express anger when there is a reasonable provocation and can express fear without hiding behind a mask of "courage."

A mature person is able to reach out for what life has to offer, even if that might mean loss.

A mature person is able to love and accept love.

And, finally, a mature person is able to see human frailty not as a betrayal, but as a reality of life.

CHAPTER IX

PUNISHMENT, A LEGITIMATE PART OF TEACHING?

As I was reading Walter R. Smith's Constructive Discipline (Smith, 1924), I discovered that two pages from his chapter on punishment were excised, cut out with a razor blade. Should such an act be punished?

We know that the old schoolmasters, those to whom White, Seeley, Cubberly, and Sears refer, would have dealt with the guilty party swiftly and, by today's standards, brutally (White, 1893; Seeley, 1903; Cubberly, 1920; Sears, 1928). They were not concerned about attaching an educational objective to punishment. Nor were they very concerned about the characteristics of effective punishment. In their minds, punishment such as pulling ears, thumping heads with thimbles, and having children kneel on peas worked, and they used it.

In their defense, however, it should be remembered that in those days, many townfolk were afraid to walk past schools for fear of being attacked; mutinies and school takeovers occurred; students as a group burned their books; and, at times, students left class en masse (Mann, 1841; Perry, 1915; Newman, 1980). Classes of 200 students were not unknown, and sometimes teachers ran away or even committed suicide (Bagley, 1926).

That's why, when I see teachers at Assertive Discipline workshops, nodding their heads in agreement with the following statement, I have to wonder about the perspectives we bring to current problems:

> Until a few years ago, the teacher was viewed in awe by both students and their parents. The teacher, simply because of her role, had respect and authority. Thus, she was a very powerful figure in the eyes of the students and could easily influence their behavior, often with just a look, a smile, or a threat (Canter & Canter, 1976).

In fairness to Canter, however, it must be noted that the 19th century school marm did have the power to expell troublemakers, and many more of her troublesome students chose to drop out. But, enough said about the good old days and how tough we have it today. Should certain behaviors be punished? The overriding question is, does it do any good to punish?

How many conformists, I wonder, would become deviates if they did not fear punishment? How many would become deviates only if they saw others getting away with behaviors they had been repressing? Are there others, so devoid of self-control and conscience, and so much a part of a subculture that they would commit crimes against society, gambling that they would never get caught, regardless of the existence of punishment? And are there still others who would never break rules (Jackson, 1964, pp. 332-337)?

The question, then, is not, should we punish, but, rather, how should we punish so that our society can be a better place to live 20 or 30 years from now?

What Should Teachers Know about Punishment?

Much of what we do know about punishment stems from research conducted with pigeons, dogs, cats, rats, and monkeys (Church, 1963, pp. 369-402). But we also know that punishment is a natural part of human existence, an important and unavoidable fact of life (Perry, 1915; Johnson, 1972, pp. 10, 33, 54). If we touch lighted coals, we frequently get burned.

We, as teachers, know that we can make a behavior worse by using the wrong kind of punishment on the wrong student. For example, if we humiliate a student in front of her peers, and their respect for her is the only basis for her self-esteem, we destroy peer control as an inhibitor.

Finally, we know why we punish. We punish to prevent further deviant behavior from the individual being punished; to sustain the morale of the conformist; to express to all that the school disapproves of the wrong being done; to neutralize the deviate as a role model; to protect other students; to make certain that everyone sees that those who do wrong cannot get ahead of those who do right; and we punish so that students will know a rule is a rule, not just a request (Sears, 1928; Coddington, 1946, pp. 115-178; Goldinger, 1974; McFatter, 1882, pp. 255-267).

In addition, we know that if we overreact and

don't consider what will help deter the individual and what will deter the group, we may punish to excess and thus provide sympathy to the offenders and justification in the minds of their peers for supporting the offender, perhaps by breaking the rules themselves.

There are also other dangers. Punishment can cause students to avoid us or activities associated or paired with the punishment. Punishment can cause retaliatory behavior, can hurt a student's self-image, can model behavior that is undesirable. If intense enough, punishment can eliminate a behavior that is both good and bad. For example, punishing a student for talking in class may cause him to terminate participation entirely. Therefore, the punishment is harmful unless we also tell the student what constitutes desirable behavior (Bandura, 1960; Vockell, 1977; Martin & Pear, 1983; Mayer et al., 1983, pp. 355-369).

Some of what we consider to be punishing, actually may be reinforcing. For example, sending students to time-out rooms may provide an opportunity for them to enjoy daydreaming, or avoid having demands placed on them.

The effectiveness of punishment depends on whether that behavior has been unintentionally rewarded in the past and for how long it has been rewarded; the age of the student; the familiarity of the offender with the punishment (Solomon, 1964, pp. 239-253); and intensity (Martin & Pear, 1983, p. 202).

Finally, we know that punishment is often cathartic for the teacher and, therefore, a reinforcer. It may also be addictive, so much so that teachers may become dependent on it and neglect other control techniques such as positive reinforcement (Martin & Pear, 1983, p. 202).

We also know that many students don't need to be punished; they just need to be told what we want, what we don't want, and what will happen if they don't comply. However, those who are disposed toward deviant behavior are prevented more by the certainty of being caught and punished than by the severity of the punishment.

Schools are this country's major civilizing

agency and should stand for morals as high as those in the best homes in America. Teachers should never lose sight of the good students that need encouragement to be good, nor of the good work done by parents that must be maintained by the school, nor that those in school now will one day live, play, and work together.

Consequences are indicative of what is right and what is wrong. Teachers should never fear making a few rules, with input from their students, and we should never hedge in enforcing rules with certainty, with fairness, and with punishment that will best help the individual and the group. A teacher's ability to match the right punishment with the right offense with the right child at the right time will influence countless others for periods far exceeding any we might imagine.

References

Bagley, William C. _School Discipline._ New York: Macmillan, 1926.

Bandura, Albert. _Principles of Behavior Modification._ New York: Holt, Rinehart, and Winston, Inc., 1969.

Canter, Lee, and Marlene Canter. _Assertive Discipline._ Los Angeles: Lee Canter and Associates, 1976.

Church, Russell M. "The Varied Effects of Punishment on Behavior." _Psychological Review_ 70 (1963): 369-402.

Coddington, F.J.O. "Problems of Punishment." _Proceedings of the Aristotelian Society_ 46 (1946): 115-178.

Cubberly, Ellwood P. _The History of Education._ Boston: Houghton Mifflin, 1920.

Goldinger, Milton, ed. _Punishment and Human Rights._ Cambridge: Schenkman Publishing Company, 1974.

Jackson, Toby. "Is Punishment Necessary?" _Journal of Criminal Law, Criminology and Police Science_ 55 (1964): 332-337.

Johnson, James M. "Punishment of Human Behavior." _American Psychologist_ 27 (1972): 10, 33, 54.

Mann, Horace. _Fourth Annual Report: Covering the Year 1840._ Boston: Dutton and Wentworth, 1841.

Martin, Garry, and Joseph Pear. _Behavior Modification: What Is It and How to Do It._ 2nd ed. New Jersey: Prentice-Hall, Inc., 1983.

Mayer, Roy G., et al. "Preventing School Vandalism and Improving Discipline: A Three-Year Study." _Journal of Applied Behavior Analysis_ 16 (1983): 355-369.

McFatter, Robert M. "Purposes of Punishment: Effects of Utilities of Criminal Sanctions on Perceived Appropriateness." _Journal of Applied Psychology_ 67 (1882): 255-267.

References

Newman, Joan. "From Past to Future: School Violence in a Broad View." Contemporary Education 52 (1980): 7-12.

Perry, Arthur C. Discipline as a School Problem. Boston: Houghton Mifflin, 1915.

Sears, Jesses B. Classroom Organization and Control. Boston: Houghton Mifflin Company, 1928.

Seeley, Levi. A New School Management. New York: Hinds and Noble, Publishers, 1903.

Smith, Walter R. Constructive School Discipline. New York: American Book Company, 1924.

Solomon, Richard L. "Punishment." American Psychologist 19 (1964): 239-253.

Vockell, Edward L. Whatev'er Happened to Punishment? Muncie: Accelerated Development, Inc., 1977.

White, Emerson E. School Management. New York: American Book Company, 1893.

CHAPTER X

SWEARING, LYING, AND CHEATING: DEVELOPING A CONCEPTUAL FRAMEWORK FROM WHICH TO REACT

Should swearing that follows a dropped lunch tray be treated the same as swearing intended to provoke? Should student backgrounds be taken into account when reacting to lying? Should knowing that even fine and decent people cheat (when they drive 69 instead of 65 on the interstate), swear (when late and the car won't start), and lie (when they say they had a great time at the boss's tea) influence our reactions?

Some teachers don't care about these "shoulds." They say cheating is cheating! Lying is lying! And foul language is foul language! All are wrong, any time, any place.

"I don't care if students know they are swearing or what word is used. I do not tolerate it! Not on any school property, for any reason. Nor do I care what provokes cheating. If their parents, gang members, and "Showtime" heroes cheat by filing false income reports, swear to appear tough and aggressive, and lie by saying the check is in the mail, that's tough; because such behaviors are offensive to me and I crush them. I tell them that swearing is immature, vulgar, and inconsiderate; lying is vicious and cowardly; and cheating is engaged in only by those too weak to live up to commitments."

Do you suppose those you hear using "Mother fu----" on the subway every day or those cutting into theater lines or those who call in false bomb threats had a teacher who "crushed" their evil tendencies?

My point? You and I cannot rid America of cheating, lying, and swearing, nor crush these behaviors out of a child. Adultery is here to stay. Plays like Edward Albee's "Who's Afraid of Virginia Wolfe" will be performed and fishermen who get the big one up to the boat and lose it will probably always swear. This does not mean we should ignore these "vices," however. But can we stop a student from engaging in these behaviors in our classroom and keep that same individual from swearing when he is walking behind our parents on a busy street; spreading vicious lies that would cost us our job or marriage; and cheating our mothers or fathers out of their life savings by selling them useless medical insurance? This, in my mind, is the question. Certainly, we can stop a student from misbehaving at school. The Gestapo proved anything can be stopped if enough fear and pain is applied. But is that our mission? By "crushing" lying, cheating, and swearing at school, while leaving attitudes unchanged, are we not just pushing these problems onto the street and community?

I believe students can learn to be considerate and can learn to only swear, lie, and cheat when and where it is appreciated. We can teach these things if we can (1) put our own values on hold; (2) remind students that even though some teachers, parents, and some presidents swear, tell white lies, and cheat on their spouses, that those who do only do so at certain times and under certain circumstances. And they never do these things to offend or deliberately hurt anyone; and (3) explain to students that to not swear when it offends, not lie when it destroys people, and not cheat when it hurts others, is just common courtesy, just good manners, just being decent.

Hard-core cases of swearing might be approached as follows: "Carol, you sure controlled the feelings of a lot of people today, myself included. But, if you want to become a master at controlling, you must be more selective about what you say and where you say it. People are afraid of confrontations and getting involved (except to page a police officer, park ranger, or another authority figure to do their reacting), so, if you really want to upset people, a lot of people, save your most vulgar swearing for a city park. If you don't see the police, just swear your heart out. Save your lying, Carol, for when you really want to annihilate someone. Start a vicious rumor and get them fired, or get them to beat up an innocent person. Or, Carol, steal someone's stuff and put it in another person's locker--someone the person being stolen from hates. Or, break into the counselor's office and change your S.A.T. scores.

"Some, however, have chosen not to go these routes. They have even been so silly as to say, 'Look, I know my gang members will turn on me and put unbelievable pressure on me, but I've got to stop this because I'm starting to feel guilty, especially when I swear around old ladies and cheat my little brothers and lie to those who trust me most.'

"And, some, Carol, have used their need for power--and that's not a dirty word; all of us need power--to become masters of themselves and their unlimited potential. I'll help. I need to improve as much as anyone. I'll help . . . ."

Admittedly, this dialogue is idealistic and, at best, could get us told where to go long before we finish; but, on the other other hand, it does make some points. It tells students we care (if we didn't, would we make the time to approach these issues in such round-about ways); that we understand and accept their right for power; that we give them credit for having a brain and want to help them see themselves as they would like to become (true, we use sarcasm, but don't send the same tired message about lying, cheating, and swearing); and it tells them how they behave is important to us, and worthy of our time. But, most importantly, it tells them we believe they have the potential to change and that they have a chance at something better in life.

CHAPTER XI

A MESSAGE FROM THOSE WHO SURVIVE

Discipline concerns most beginning teachers. This is because 30 students can break a teacher and because most classes contain enough masters of disobedience and defiance to make any teacher's life unpleasant. Against such odds, it's surprising first-year teachers survive. Fortunately, most do. This chapter is an edited sampling of their advice.

#1   I have survived because I get to know my students. I learn their names the first day. Any college graduate who thinks it is important enough and makes sure he hears the name correctly in the first place can do it. I also learn their special interests (using a questionnaire, if necessary) and relate classroom activities to those interests. It's hard for students to be mean to someone who cares about them.

#2   If I use punishment, I make sure it is punishment. If a child needs to be sent to detention more than once, detention is a reward--a place to meet friends, a way to avoid troubles on the bus, etc.-- not a punishment.

#3   I am organized, have high expectations, and run class in a business-like manner.

#4   I make sure each student succeeds at what is being done--even if I have to create materials. To expect students to work at something over their heads, without even a chance at success, is the real "cruel and unusual punishment."

#5   I respect and encourage individual differences. I enjoy those who, in a reasoned, civil way, challenge the status quo, dare to think differently, and refuse to follow along like sheep. I think I would have enjoyed rebels like H.K. Mencken, Upton Sinclair, and Thomas Paine as students.

#6   I have survived because I haven't expected much from administrators. I'd like them to ask my advice, care about what I believe, and respect me. But, I can live without their attention.

I matter, and what I do matters. I may not be

paid or respected as much as they are, but I'm just as important! I have as much interest in and concern for the school and its students as anyone, and my opinion is every bit as important as anyone's.

I'll work with administrators that are fair, open, and positive. But I have only contempt for those who have pets, listen to favorites, and talk about teachers to other teachers "behind closed doors."

#7   Parents may swear, ignore notices, or hang up the telephone--but they care nonetheless. I've survived because I believe this. I may have to say, "We both want what's best for Sara, what if we try . . . ." many times; but, if I say it often enough, blaming and defensiveness stop and cooperation begins.

#8   I find something in every child to like. At times, this is most difficult. But, if I talk and listen long enough, I can always discover something to admire, appreciate, respect, or enjoy about each child.

#9   I have survived because I frequently remind myself that the main difference between students in my classes and juveniles in serious trouble or even in state correctional facilities is that those in my class had, when it was needed, someone to talk to. I try to be a person my students trust enough to talk to.

#10   I have survived because I don't pussyfoot around. I make it known that certain behaviors are wrong. No one wants to be called self-righteous, holier than thou, or narrow minded, but I take stands anyway. As a teacher, my assessment of a student's behavior is still the best predictor there is for determining future delinquency (Jessor & Jessor, 1977), so I call them as I see them.

#11   And, finally, I have survived because I spend extra time with and have greater patience for children who: (1) are impatient, impulsive, and fail to listen to instructions; (2) exercise poor judgment and fail to reflect upon past performance; (3) make self-centered verbal responses, interrupt others, blurt out personal thoughts, and make irrelevant comments during ongoing discussions; and (4) become involved in excessive talking, poking, and noise

making.   I do this because research has shown that
these are behavior patterns of children most likely to
get   into serious trouble later on (National Institute
for Juvenile Justice and Delinquency Prevention).

Survivors   know what to reward, get to know their
students,   are organized,   provide students   with
success,   have pride in themselves,   find something in
every child to like, know what is normal, and are
aware of what behaviors, if continued, get children
into trouble with the authorities later in life.

References

Jessor, J., and S.L. Jessor. <u>Problem Behavior and Psychological Development</u>. New York: Academic Press, 1977.

National Institute for Juvenile Justice and Delinquency Prevention. <u>1983-84 Blue Report of N.I.J.J.D.P.</u> Washington, D.C.

CHAPTER XII

MODELS OF DISCIPLINE

One way of disciplining will not work for all children. Yelling controls some, but terrifies most. Spanking shapes up a few, but traumatizes others. Touching is liked by many, but a few detest it. Most methods of discipline will work for most children, but none will work for all children. This is an important point, because when we discuss models, I do not want you to think a panacea exists. When it comes to discipline, there are no experts.

A model of discipline is simply its creator's theory or system of discipline, his or her way of approaching discipline problems. There are thousands of models of discipline, as many as there are teachers. Only a few of these models, however, have become well known.

We will concentrate upon six of them--Lee Canter's "Assertive Discipline"; William Glasser's "Reality Therapy"; Thomas Gordon's "Teacher Effectiveness Training"; Alfred Alschuler's "Social Literacy Training"; James Dobson's "Dare to Discipline"; and Rudolf Dreikurs' "Discipline without Tears."

Information on other models such as Transactional Analysis; Vorrath's Positive Peer Culture; Behavor Modification; Duke's Supplematic Management Plan for School Discipline; the Kounin Model; the Redl and Wallenberg Model; the Jones Model; Richard M. Mallory's the Least Approach to Classroom Discipline; the Gnagey Model; the Brophy Model; the Ginott Model; the Randy Sprick Model, etc., is available in materials in the selected Bibliography.

Lee Canter's Assertive Discipline may be the best known and most widely used model of discipline. Mr. Canter, a former elementary teacher and specialist in child guidance, studied successful teachers; then, with his wife Marlene, created a model based upon what successful teachers do to get order.

His model is rather simple: If students obey the rules and do not disrupt the learning process, they get rewarded. If, however, they disobey the rules and disrupt the learning process, they get punished.

63

In Canter's plan, the teacher is boss. The children are told the classroom rules, usually not more than five, and are told that no one will be allowed to break them. They are also told that no students, for any reason, will be allowed to keep the teacher from teaching, nor other classmates from learning. If a student misbehaves, they are told their name will go on the board. They are also told that if they behave, they will get a reward. A note explaining this program goes home to every parent.

Once the Canter model is in place, if a child breaks a rule, his or her name is written on the board. This is done calmly without anger and without disrupting the class. It is done simply to provide a warning. If a child misbehaves a second time, a check goes behind the name. This means 15 minutes after school. If the child misbehaves again, another check goes behind the name. This means 30 minutes after school. If the child misbehaves again, another check goes up and a note goes home to the parent. If a fourth check is necessary in one period, this means seeing the principal. Students, of course, know what each check means and, thus, can decide if they want punishment and, if so, how much punishment they want.

If students are good, however, and follow the rules--raise their hands, stay in their seats, follow directions, keep hands, feet, and objects to themselves, and come to class on time--they will get a reward. Sometimes a marble is dropped into a jar for good behaviors. When enough marbles are accumulated, perhaps a party or other pleasant activity is held on a Friday.

Lee Canter's model trains teachers to look for the positive, raise what they are doing from the intuitive to the conscious level, clearly and firmly communicate their wants to students, and prepare themselves to back up what they say.

Being the best known has also made Canter's model the most open to attack. Some believe he is ill-informed when he suggests that all children can be good if they want to, insensitive when he gives rights only to teachers, naive when he fails to acknowledge a certain amount of movement and rebellion is normal, and has his head in the clouds for not realizing his model only somewhat works at the middle school and is a joke in high schools.

Obviously, Mr. Canter doesn't believe children should be trained as animals, nor treated as if they were in a prison camp. Nor does he believe that when students leave school, and the rewards and punishments stop, that they will become beasts. He realizes his model will not match every teaching style, and that students can't have all their problems solved by the teachers and then be expected to solve their own when they graduate.

His model seems to work well for those students who know right from wrong and want to do what they should, but lack the ability to discipline themselves.

One caution? Once a group of graduate students in my discipline class asked their second and third graders what punishment they most feared. You guessed it! The number one fear, by far, was having their name put on the board.

William Glasser, a psychiatrist and prolific writer, created the Reality Therapy Approach to discipline while working with delinquent girls at a California residential treatment center. Basically, Glasser believes teachers should help youngsters: (1) see themselves as others see them; (2) help children make judgments about whether their behavior is helping or hurting themselves; (3) help students accept reality as it actually is, rather than as they would like it to be; (4) help students see the need for change and make a plan for changing; and (5) check frequently to see if the students are following through with their commitment to change. Self-understanding, self-discipline, understanding the power of choice, and not making excuses and blaming the past for present behavior are key end products of Glasser's model.

In a school setting, Glasser would first ask that teachers create an environment friendly to students-- an environment that would accept students, help them see that they can have some control over their own lives, and one that would help them derive a feeling of satisfaction for being in school. He would ask this because he believes that seldom do people cause problems when they are where they want to be.

In school, Glasser would ask that each teacher pursue each problem in the following order.

First, ask the students what's happening. Ask, "What are you doing?" If the student didn't know what she was doing, Glasser would tell her what she was doing.

Second, Glasser would ask, "Is it doing you any good? Is it helping you?" If the student thought it was helping them, Glasser would explain how he and others perceive the behavior.

Third, if the child could see the behavior was counterproductive, Glasser would ask him to make a plan to do something about it. If the child couldn't make a plan, Glasser would suggest two or three possibilities.

Fourth, Glasser would check to see if the plan was working and would not accept any excuses if it was not as yet accomplished. "You said you were going to do it. When are you going to do it? What can I do to help you accomplish your plan?"

In summary, under Glasser's model, you help children see that there is hope, see that their behavior may be keeping them from achieving this hope, and see that they can control their own behavior. And you help them make a judgment about their behavior, get them to make a plan for changing their behavior, and you check to see if they are following through. You don't punish and you don't accept excuses.

Glasser's model doesn't get much criticism. That's probably because it's hard to fault anyone who wants people to achieve better self-discipline. Its main weakness is in how it is carried out. If a teacher forces a student to develop a plan or makes a plan for a student before that student acknowledges a problem exists or sees a need for change, or seriously wants to change, the model crumples at this point. All hinges on helping the student believe a change is in his or her best interests. It's pretty hard to stop a kid from guarding a crack house or dealing and stealing when his peers praise him for such behavior, when he is able to drive a new car, and when he is able to have his pick of girls. The down side may not impress him, because his friends who have gone to prison not only were not raped, but emerged with even higher status.

Thomas Gordon, a clinical psychologist, might

well have called his Teacher Effectiveness Training Model the "no-lose democratic approach to problem resolution model." Many believe his model, based on Carl Rogers' nondirective counseling theory, shows the most promise, but also is the most idealistic of the six we will discuss.

Gordon's overall message is very student centered. He believes that students should learn to govern themselves, and that in a warm, open, understanding, nonjudgmental environment, a student will choose what is best for himself. Thus, if a student has a problem, the teacher should listen actively, feel empathy--not sympathy, and do all possible to hold a mirror up to the student. In such an environment, a student will do what is best.

Gordon believes it is inappropriate in a democratic society for a teacher to decide all solutions to all problems. But, he also believes that a teacher cannot remain sane nor keep his job if he is so permissive as to give in to all student whims and demands. The solution he suggests is for students and teachers to work together to find satisfactory solutions to classroom problems.

If a teacher is upset, she should not blame, bully, or browbeat and say, "You kids are rotten." She should instead send an I message, such as, "I am very upset. I am trying to teach, but I can't hear myself think." This doesn't put anyone on the defensive. Instead, it asks for help and gives some responsibility to the students.

In summary, Gordon believes teachers should respect students, listen to them, and ask for their help in resolving problems. In addition, he believes that teachers should use the pronoun "I" instead of "you"; and that rewards and punishment do more harm than good, because they make students slaves to authority and do nothing to develop independence.

Although it is hard to argue against encouraging more mutual respect and civility, Gordon is often put down by experienced teachers, because they say children are too young to listen to reason; that in the real world, kids do not make the best discussions, even in a humane environment; and that there isn't time to listen to every kid with a problem. They all seem to agree, however, that "I" messages save them a

67

lot of grief and backtalk.

Alfred Alschuler, a clinical psychologist and college teacher, created the <u>Social Literacy Training Model</u>. It is based upon the work of the humanist Brazilian educator, Paulo Freire. It is the least known of the models we'll discuss, possibly because it is the newest.

Alschuler asks teachers and administrators to look beyond the individuals when recurring problems arise, i.e., if children are constantly running in the halls after school, look at the time school dismisses as opposed to when the buses leave. Don't just assume getting more teachers to patrol the halls will help. Alschuler is concerned that when we look for causes of discipline problems, that we don't always look first at the student and then at the teacher. He suggests that we also look for plausible causes in the system of schooling--that is, at the rules, roles, and goals of the school where we teach.

A basic credo of the Social Literacy Model is that if we always blame persons for the problem, we not only overlook root system causes--i.e., outdated rules, misunderstood roles, oppressive goals, false norms, etc.--but we also make false assumptions about the very people with whom we need to communicate.

When you experience conflict, Alschuler suggests that you try saying to yourself:

1. My needs are legitimate. Other people's needs are legitimate, too, even though we are in conflict and even though I may not be sure what their needs really are.

2. This conflict is not unique. I'm sure other people are having similar problems. There is a pattern, though I may not see it now.

3. It is possible to find a way for all of our needs to be met without conflict, though I may not know that solution now.

4. We're playing a game, and it is to blame for the pattern of conflict. We need to change the rules and roles, not the players.

5. As an individual, I cannot figure this out

and solve it alone. I need to talk with other teachers or students or administrators to name the game, the rules, the roles, the needs. I need the cooperation of others to resolve this pattern of conflict and play a new game in which we can all win.

In summary, Alschuler's Social Literacy Training Model tries to discourage teachers and students from blaming each other for their problems. Instead, he encourages teachers and students to communicate openly, honestly, and frequently, and perceive classroom management as a joint enterprise.

He believes that role playing would help each party see the problem from a different view, and he believes brainstorming patterns of conflict and involvement in conflict resolution would be helpful.

I believe the model has great promise, primarily because it encourages us to stop the blaming and start discussing what role the system--the way we've always done things--has had in making us all feel oppressed.

James Dobson is given credit for making the <u>Dare to Discipline Model</u> popular. Dobson taught for a short time in a public school, studied to become a psychologist, and now is deeply involved in scripture study and church-related activities. His model is extremely popular among today's parents. As one parent put it, "I love Dr. Dobson. Now I don't have to feel guilty about clobbering my kid anymore!"

Dobson believes the first day of teaching is the most important day of the year. He believes that it is important to students to know who is the toughest, and he believes a teacher should perhaps even create opportunities to show they are in charge and will do what is necessary to maintain order.

Authority is necessary, says Dobson. It is not a negative word. Students need and want discipline and are secure only in an environment with clearly defined rules and limits. Small problems remain small if you catch them promptly and deal with them firmly. He believes that although anger doesn't get a teacher anywhere, not smiling until Thanksgiving might well help the beginning teacher. In addition, he believes it is important for teachers to get to know students, to respect students, and to let students know, after a confrontation, that you still care about them.

An education student having not yet student taught might perceive Dobson as an oppressive, authoritarian dictator--at least, many tell me this. But, veteran teachers like him. This alarms me a little, possibly because we live in a pluralistic democracy and I think we should graduate students who possess a little self-discipline. The other side, of course, is that if you don't have order, you don't have anything--not indoctrination, coercion, brainwashing, S-R conditioning--nothing.

In summary, Dobson takes us back to the late 1890s and early 1900s, when teaching politeness, manners, morals, citizenship, and respect for authority were part of the curriculum. At that time, rudeness, willful disobedience, and incivility were not tolerated, and physical contact was a solution to these problems. Dobson believes permissiveness has caused many of today's problems.

Rudolf Dreikurs created the Logical Consequences Model of Discipline. It is the oldest model we will discuss.

Few teachers know about Rudolf Dreikurs, an Austrian born in 1897, but nearly all have heard of the late Dreikurs' ideas. This is because scores of presenters, consultants, and authors have reworked the Dreikurs model and have then presented it as their own, and because much of Dreikurs' own work is rooted in the ideas of the famous Alfred Adler.

Dreikurs' model contains three major thrusts. In thrust one, Dreikurs presents his major beliefs. (We will note 17 of them.) In thrust two, he explains natural and logical consequences. And in thrust three, he discusses the four, and only four, reasons children misbehave, when they fail to gain a feeling of belonging, a sense of significance or the status, recognition, and acceptance they desire from the group.

Thrust One: Seventeen Beliefs of Dreikurs

1. Teachers need to understand that children have been given freedom in our society without learning an accompanying sense of responsibility.

2. Teachers must learn to be democratic leaders and see power, pressure, and punishment for what they

are--relics of the feudal past.

3. Most of our problem teenagers are living in an arrested state of infantile selfishness with no developed sense of responsibility toward a task, or their fellow men.

4. Discipline is the seed from which freedom grows.

5. Nagging, preaching, repeating directions, and criticizing are an absolute waste of "air" time. Where discipline is concerned, you know that quiet action is always more effective than words.

6. Any child who has the teacher, principal, and school psychologist all upset deserves a certain amount of credit.

7. Leaders of juvenile gangs see the whole society as their enemy and frequently look down on others with contempt. Yet, underneath the facade, they are deeply discouraged individuals with little hope for themselves.

8. No child would switch to the socially unacceptable side of life if he were not discouraged. He believes that he has no place in the group and can't succeed with useful means; therefore, he is discouraged--and the terrible circle is continued. Democratic teachers have the power to break that vicious circle.

9. Separate the deed from the doer. One may reject the child's actions without rejecting the child.

10. Remember that genuine happiness comes from self-sufficiency: children need to learn to take care of themselves.

11. Children don't need bribes to be good. They actually want to be good.

12. Punishment is only effective for those who don't need it.

13. Students should always be allowed input into establishing rules. And they should always understand the reasons for rules.

14. Praise can be terribly discouraging. Encouragement, however, stimulates the effort and fastens attention upon one's capacity to join humanity, and also to become aware of interior strength and ability to cope. Teachers should be alert for opportunities to recognize effort.

15. The system of rewarding children for good behavior is as detrimental as the system of punishment.

16. A disobedient child is always a domineering child.

17. Children prefer being scolded, punished, and even beaten to being ignored.

Thrust Two: Logical and Natural Consequences

Dreikurs believes that punishment doesn't teach anything today, and that the democratic teacher uses logical consequences instead. By using consequences instead of punishment, the teacher allows reality to replace the authority of the adult. All of us can think of hundreds of examples of results that follow certain behaviors, i.e., if the milk is not put away at night, it is spoiled the next morning; if we run a red light, we often get hit by another car, etc.-- these are natural consequences.

In the school setting, sometimes consequences are arranged by the teacher. These are called logical consequences. If children don't turn in work, they get poorer grades; if they are late, they have to make up the time at recess or after school; if they forget a pencil, they have to write with a very short one provided by the teacher; if they don't pay their fines, they don't get their grades; if they break windows, they have to replace them; if they are fighting during recess, they don't get recess; if a child is not listening in a reading lesson, she will miss her turn to read orally, etc.

Dreikurs believes that if logical consequences bear a direct relationship to the behavior and are understood by students, they will teach students that good behavior brings rewards and unacceptable behavior brings unpleasant consequences. Teachers don't need to be vindictive or oppressive. They just need to calmly and in the manner of a mature adult, provide the consequence. If the child chooses to behave, the consequence given is a good one; if not, the consequence is a negative one.

Thrust Three: The Four Ways Children Misbehave

We have all heard about the only child being different, how the first born is different from the baby of the family, and how the middle child is different from all the above. These ideas come from Adler and Dreikurs. Dreikurs observed hundreds of misbehaving children and determined that they misbehaved for one of these four reasons (he challenged anyone to come up with any reason other than these four): (1) to get attention; (2) to demonstrate power and superiority; (3) to retaliate or seek revenge for feeling hurt; and (4) to protect themselves from more humiliation and embarrassment. (This last one is accomplished by becoming totally passive.)

The reason Dreikurs' ideas about why kids misbehave (to get attention, power, revenge, and to display inadequacy), are important is because he believes none of these behaviors get a child anywhere. They are, in fact, counterproductive in every way. Yet, these very behaviors get a teacher's attention every time. And what does attention do to undesirable behavior? Of course, it increases it. So, Dreikurs is telling us to ignore power struggles, bids for attention, revenge-seeking activities, and displays of inadequacy,

It is important at this point to briefly digress for a moment. Children need to feel a part of the group. If they are accepted, if their useful contributions and conformity to the requirements of the group make them feel a part of the group, make them feel accepted and give them status, they will continue such behaviors and become students who: think in terms of "we" rather than just "I"; respect the rights of others; are tolerant of others; are willing to share, rather than being concerned with "how much can I get"; are honest and put forth genuine effort. Only if a child is accepted will she use constructive methods.

If, however, these behaviors do not bring acceptance, if they do not help him find his place in the world, the child will try different behaviors to get this acceptance. What they find effective, they will continue to use. The behaviors that meet their needs best will be kept. All of their behavior has a purpose, and if their attempts to get status from adults via the positive way fails, they will try other ways. These other ways, such as displaying inadequacy, revenge, power, or attention getting, in the child's mind are logical and should succeed in getting the acceptance they need; but, of course, to adults, they are seen as negative. Frequently, a discouraged child, which is what an unaccepted child is, will become consumed by the need for self-elevation.

Let's now go back to the four goals of children's misbehavior, the four behaviors Dreikurs says we should extinguish. The four goals that continue only because the child falsely believes that these particular misbehaviors will give the social acceptance he or she deserves.

Dreikurs believes we must modify these behaviors, not only because hateful, cruel actions annoy us, but, as stated earlier, because they don't do anything for the child, either. But, he adds, modifying just the behaviors won't do. If we want our involvement to do any lasting good, we must also modify the motivation behind the behavior. How? By helping the student recognize why she is behaving in this manner.

Ah, but how do we know if they want power or just attention, or if they want revenge? Believe it or not, this is the most simple part of all. Just ask, how you feel. If you feel annoyed, the child wants attention; if you feel defeated or threatened, the child wants power; if you feel deeply hurt, it's revenge; and if you feel helpless, the child wants to escape and is demonstrating hopelessness.

Once you determine your own feelings--thus, the motivation behind the child's behavior--you confront them with it. You ask for what purpose are they behaving this way. You do not criticize, or make judgments, or behave angrily or emotionally. You simply say: (1) "Could it be you want special attention?"; (2) "Could it be that you want your own way and hope to be boss?"; (3) "Could it be that you want to hurt others as much as you feel hurt by them?"; (4) "Could it be that you want to be left alone?" You always ask all four questions because the

74

child may be operating on more than one level. You tell at what level they are on by the answer given and the recognition reflex you see, i.e., his mouth says "no," but his nose says "yes"; the roguish smile; a twinkle of the eyes; or the twitch of a facial muscle. Sometimes it is so obvious the child covers her face or bursts into laughter.

Sometimes the confrontation itself helps the child to change. If not, the teacher is encouraged to use logical consequences, encouragement, or finding a "buddy" in the same group. Class discussions are also encouraged. Even the most discouraged child can be helped.

Dreikurs' ideas are probably not new to you, nor does it take a genius to figure out that this model would take time to use; but, it does seem to have merit. It does, if for no other reason than because it makes us realize how important it is for us to make children feel they belong and for us to encourage them. This model works best for children 10 and under, but many junior high, middle school, and 9th and 10th grade teachers tell me it works for them, as well. It helps them open communications between themselves and their students; it removes the fun students get from provoking the teacher; and it stops misbehavior, thus giving the teacher a chance to redirect it. Keep in mind that students cannot be involved in power struggles with themselves.

If teachers don't do what's in the best long-run interests of the child, probably no one will--at least, - that is a safe assumption, since the problem still exists. Dreikurs' model is the most complicated of the six discussed, but it has much to offer. Every teacher, regardless of philosophy, can gain sound advice from it.

CHAPTER XIII

WE HAVE SUPPORT TO DO THE JOB WE NEED TO DO!

How do we know something is good, moral, or righteous? Who decides these things? The local newspaper editor? Those who tell police what to ignore? The dominant ones at coffee break? Those most passionate about scripture interpretation?

As a teacher, I encourage you to examine all sources of rules, but especially those that impact what you discipline and how you discipline. Some rules and the punishment dealt out for breaking them are simply silly. But some rules are rooted in tradition and law, especially rules based upon U.S. Supreme Court decisions. These are the rules I invite you to carefully examine.

"Do that and I'll sue you." "Touch me and you'll be jerked into court so fast your head will swim." "Oh, we can't do that; we'd have parents and lawyers beating our doors down." Sound familiar?

Just remember, anybody can sue anybody for most anything. There are a lot of kooks out there, and some of them have lawyers. Considering that we live in an extremely, if not obsessively, litigious society, I'm amazed we don't get sued more often. And, I'm especially amazed that the parents of one child don't more frequently sue the parents of another child! Children put tacks on the chairs of other children, snap them with rubber bands, and put their coats in toilets. They intimidate shy children to the point of making them reluctant to come to school, and they disrupt classes, causing some children not to learn. Why don't parents sue each other more often? Possibly because we act as a buffer.

When a parent is not around to protect her child from humiliation and from being hurt; when a parent is not around to keep the few from interrupting her child's learning, who must fill the void? Right. The teacher. But do teachers have the power to step in? You bet we do!

In spite of half-truths to the contrary, we have the ultimate power in our corner! The Supreme Court of the United States is behind us all the way! All the Supreme Court has always asked is would a mature,

reasonable, responsible person have reacted as you
did? They have consistently used as a guide: Would a
prudent person have done what you did; would a
responsible person under the same circumstances have
done the same thing? The Supreme Court knows you
cannot teach without control.

Starting with Tinker v. Des Moines Independent
Community School District 393 (1969) through Baker v.
Owen (44 USLW 3237 1975) and Ingraham v. Wright (1977)
and ending with New Jersey v. T.L.O. (1985) and
Hazelwood School District v. Kuhlmeier (1988), the
Supreme Court has sided in most cases with teachers
and administrators.

Yes, they said students have rights, i.e., the
opportunity to tell their side; to know what they are
accused of; to be forewarned if the punishment is to
be a paddling (unless the behavior really shocks the
conscience); and to not have a search be unduly
intrusive (a strip search). But, at the same time,
they made it perfectly clear that no one has the right
to materially and/or substantially disrupt the
discipline and operation of the schools.

The justices of the U.S. Supreme Court know the
future of our nation rests with the schools. They
believe the schools have a duty to teach "the habits
and manners of civility" (Minneapolis Star Tribune,
July 8, 1986, p. 5A).

The U.S. Supreme Court justices have done all
they can to support an environment that will allow
learning to occur. In fact, some say they have gone
too far. We can search school property (lockers); we
can search students (New Jersey v. T.L.O., January
1985); we can suspend students who use vulgar language
(Minneapolis Star Tribune, July 8, 1986, p. 5A); we
can defend ourselves; we can prohibit deliberately
disruptive noise outside of school buildings when
school is in session; suspend a student immediately if
his or her behavior poses an immediate threat to
persons, property, or the academic process; we can
control the content of school-sponsored publications,
dramatic productions, and other expressive school
activities (Legal Update, Winter 1988, p. 33); and we
can even paddle students in the absence of a state or
district statute against it.

Join A.F.T. or N.E.A.; get your $1,000,000+

liability insurance. It can't hurt. But, don't overreact to the "do that and I'll sue you" routine. At the Supreme Court level, you have all the support you need to do the job you need to do. One caution, however; although the Supreme Court is solidly behind teachers and has been fair to teachers and administrators, lower courts are sometimes not so generous. Frequently, they are swayed by arguments the Supreme Court would quickly dismiss.

U.S. Supreme Court Cases

1. Tinker v. Des Moines

The U.S. Supreme Court ruled in favor of three Quaker children in Iowa who had been suspended from school in 1965 for wearing black arm bands. They added that schools should not be totalitarian and that students are persons who do not shed their rights at the school gates.

2. Baker v. Owen (1975)

The U.S. Supreme Court affirmed the decision of the lower court that school officials could employ corporal punishment (spanking), over the objections of parents, to restrain or correct pupils and to maintain order. They must, however, warn the student that if they continue to misbehave, corporal punishment will be used; not use it as the first line of punishment; and, if repeated, send a written explanation of the punishment to the child's parents.

3. Ingraham v. Wright (Dade County, Florida)

A. On October 6, 1970, James Ingraham and Roosevelt Andrews, students at Drew Junior High School in Miami, responded slowly to a teacher's order.

B. They were taken to the principal's office and held over the desk and given 20 whacks with a two-feet long, four-inches wide, one-half-inch-thick paddle.

C. Ashamed, James showed his injuries; his posterior was black and purple.

D. The injuries were diagnosed as "hematoma" requiring pain pills, ice packs, and rest at home for a week.

Eleven days of school were missed, and a physician's attention was required.

E.   Co-plaintiff Roosevelt Andrews was also paddled.

F.   Although his father protested, the paddlings continued.

G.   Roosevelt on one occasion loses the full use of his wrist and arm for a week.

H.   Review by the U.S. Supreme Court was granted to Ingraham on May 24, 1976.

Result: In the Ingraham v. Wright case, on April 19, 1977, the U.S. Supreme Court, by a 5-4 vote, ruled that the punishment meted out to the petitioners did not violate the Eighth Amendment ban against cruel and unusual punishment, nor did it violate the due process clause of the Fourteenth Amendment.

4.   New Jersey v. T.L.O.

Terry Lee Owens, 14, of Picataway, New Jersey, was accused of smoking in the rest room. The vice principal searched her purse. The court ruled that if schools have reasonable grounds for search and are not excessively intrusive (cavity or strip searches are not allowed), they can search, and that the evidence found is admissible in a juvenile court delinquency hearing.

5.   Hazelwood School District v. Kuhlmeier (January 1988)

The Hazelwood case concerns a newspaper written and edited by a Missouri high school journalism class as part of the school's curriculum. The school principal deleted two stories written by students-- one dealing with student pregnancy, and the other discussing divorce--because he felt there was not enough time to make needed changes (to protect identities) before publication. The court sided with the principal and declared that a school need not tolerate student speech which is inconsistent with the educational mission.

References

Legal   Update.   "Court   Upholds   School   Paper's
     Censorship." School Safety (Winter 1988): 33.

Minneapolis Star Tribune. 8 July 1986: 5A.

CHAPTER XIV

ROLE PLAYING AND DISCIPLINE

You are sitting in a crowded theater trying to enjoy your escape, but the couple behind you keeps talking. The more they talk, the angrier they get. Soon you find yourself more involved in giving them dirty looks than you are with the movie. How might this dilemma be resolved?

Unlike heroes on television who solve such dilemmas with poise, grace, and perhaps even humor, in real life many of us do not. In fact, we often leave such situations muttering that we should have said something other than we did, or should not have said anything.

Role playing can help us move away from self-condemning mutterings and toward reactions that allow us to feel better about ourselves. By role playing situations with a high likelihood of occurring in our lives, we can internalize the fact that we have some control over our actions and reactions. We can also see how effective our responses appear to be.

When using role playing, a few guidelines are necessary: (1) Role-playing situations should be kept brief, not more than two or three minutes; otherwise, too many issues surface and processing becomes difficult. (2) It is not necessary for individuals to portray themselves; in fact, playing the part of a person of the opposite sex or of a different age could help them gain insights into others. (3) Anything that adds a little realism is helpful. In the case of the movie situation, part of the room might be arranged to look like a movie theater. And (4) Psych time is also important. For instance, each "movie" couple should be taken aside and given instructions and time to get into the role. The couple watching the movie might be asked what theater they are in, and what bothers them about people who talk in movies. The "talkers" could be asked where they have just been, where they are going after the movie, and why it is impossible for them to enjoy a movie unless they can share their thoughts and feelings as they are experiencing them.

For role playing to be successful, an atmosphere of trust must exist. No one should be forced to role play, and every effort, especially at first, must be rewarded. In addition, it is important for everyone to realize that the players are not themselves, but, for a few moments, are acting a part.

After the role-play situation has completed, both those viewing and those playing a role should be given a chance to talk about their experience. Questions such as, "Has this ever happened to you?," or, "How else might this have been handled?," should generate some response. The important thing to remember when discussing a role-playing situation is that no one should ever be allowed to criticize the person who played a role.

Once everyone learns what role playing is and what guidelines to follow, role playing can occur spontaneously. Imagine, for example, that you are discussing suicide and someone asks, "Well, how should you react when someone says he's had it and is going to drive his car off a bridge?" This dialogue could be quickly role played and the alternative responses discussed.

What follows are incidents you and your class members or colleagues might role play and discuss.

Incident #1

You are in an adult evening class from 6 p.m. until 8 p.m. There is a woman in your class who is not only eight months pregnant, but also very fat, actually obese. Every evening she eats Twinkies and taco chips and drinks Diet Pepsi. She also smokes cigarettes, almost a pack during the two-hour period. Watching this woman and hearing her talk about her baby, you can barely keep from telling her to be more considerate of that child--especially to stop smoking! You never say anything because you don't know how to do it tactfully.

Incident #2

It is time for homeroom announcements and a junior high boy is asked to sit down at his desk. Instead of doing so, he lies down on the floor. What would you do?

Incident #3

A high school boy was caught watering some plants in the room wth Xerox solution in order to kill the plants. What should be done to him?

Incident #4

A high school teacher is assigned lunchroom duty for elementary students. The teacher hates the assignment and adopts harsh rules for the students. One day after lunch, my students came to me very upset about the teacher in the lunchroom. I do not express approval or disapproval--just listen. I encourage the students to share their feelings with the lunchroom teacher, which they do. The lunchroom teacher tells the students, "You tell your teacher to mind her own damn business!" That night the teacher calls me and swears for 10 minutes, then hangs up.

Incident #5

This incident occurred in my first year of teaching around Halloween. My mobile home, which was located directly adjacent to the school, received a good pelting of tomatoes. Naturally, the treatment irritated me, and I reacted in the following way. I had an idea of who was involved, and I let it be known that if my mobile home and the area around it were not cleaned up, I would make the chemistry course or class regret it by really piling on the work. The class knew how hard the work could get, and they knew I meant it. By the end of school that day, my mobile home and the ground around it were cleaned up immaculately--better than before.

Incident #6

I enjoy laughing with the students, but sometimes it only provokes them further to do "funny" things. A student sat in the back of the room and faced the back, his glasses on backwards. I laughed, and soon several were immitating him.

Incident #7

A co-worker allows her children to be rowdy in the halls, bang their locker doors, talk loudly in the halls, squeak their shoes when they walk, and other negative behaviors. She is standing right by them in the hall and says nothing. What, if anything, should I do to correct the situation without causing hard feelings and/or embarrassment to the teacher and probably to myself?

Incident #8

While supervising the lunchroom for the first time, some peas went sailing from one table to another! I went over and asked the table being thrown at who had been the culprit, but no one would "squeal." I then walked over to the principal, who was also in the lunchroom, and explained the situation and told him the whole table should be suspended from the lunchroom until someone would own up to the incident. He [the principal] said I couldn't kick 12 people out and must catch the student in the <u>act</u> before suspending him from lunch.

Incident #9

A first grader's parents have recently separated. The girl presently lives with her mother and grandmother, and the girl's father lives in another town. The father is suicidal and is seeking therapy. Although the mother is absolutely positive that she will terminate the marriage, the father has convinced the child that he will be home soon. The child is very frustrated in school, cannot concentrate on her work, and is falling behind in all subjects. Despite efforts of the mother to help the child realize the separation is final, the child refuses to accept it. How is this unproductive and bitter child to be handled in the classroom?

Incident #10

An upcoming eighth grade class for 1984-85 has 12 students, at least, that have given their previous teachers nightmares since kindergarten. For example, one boy has the knack of going home and telling lies to his mother. His mother reacts very violently; she may phone the school and swear at the teacher or the principal; or she may come to the school and swear at the teacher(s). In fact, three years ago in the elementary area, she did come to the school and created a ruckus; the administration signed a complaint and restraining order forbidding her entry to the school unless she was invited. Her son, it appears, intentionally tells lies to get her to react;

then he sits back and watches the fireworks. What would you do?

Incident #11

Small students sometimes become the target of the large bully in the class. I walked into the sixth grade class one morning and found that the large boy had the small student on his knees, repeating phrases and generally humiliating him. How would you handle this situation?

Incident #12

I had this student that was really becoming a behavior problem. I called a parent and wished to share that day's incident and try to make a team effort with the parent to solve the situation. But, I was surprised to have the parent tell me that the child was my problem from 8 to 3. Outside of that, she would deal with the child.

Incident #13

One problem at our high school that we have is heavy kissing in the halls, and, as teachers, we have been asked to comment about the situation to the students, when we see it. Well, I commented to a couple who I caught in the act! My words were: "Don't you think that there is another place to do this other than the school?" The boy responded: "Is your room open? Or, better yet, can we have the key to it so we can lock it?" The school has called the parents about the situation; however, this doesn't help the situation. What can you do as teachers if there is really no school policy about this situation?

Incident #14

Whenever our school is involved in a state tournament, our teachers are asked if they attend a game, the administration would like them to act as supervisors. The visibility of these teachers supposedly will discourage inappropriate behavior. During one of these games, I sat next to boys that were not from my school. They were using obscene and abusive language. My children were also with me. I finally decided to say something, mainly because I didn't want my kids to hear this type of language. If my kids would not have been with me, should I have said something to these kids, even though they weren't from my school?

Incident #15

A student is angry at his local grocery store owner who fired his brother because the brother was a poor worker. The student, in relating the incident, refers to the owner as a cheap "Jewboy." How does the teacher respond to this remark? Does he ignore it?

Incident #16

After allowing a student to go to the library, within 10 minutes he sauntered into the room with a long cattail suggestively swinging between his legs.

Incident #17

The general climate of our sixth grade has been destroyed this past year by one sixth grade girl. She has sufficient social power to involve her circle of friends in various hurtful acts towards persons outside this group. Her activities in this area include such things as "Let's hate Laurie this week," sabotaging birthday parties with either a general boycott or rude and inappropriate behavior while at the party, and hate phone calls to one new student. These calls numbered over 25 during one weekend and most frequently included threats on the life of the new student. The parents of the behavior-problem child back the girl to the nth degree and insist their child would not consider doing these things.

Incident #18

My husband was at a mechanic's shop in town when the mechanic's son came in with a group of four-five boys from my class. He told the boys and my husband how he had slapped me in physical education because he didn't want to do the activity. He further stated I left the room crying and did not return. Nothing had even happened. What should I have done the next class period with him?

Incident #19

I had noon hour supervision for high school students. Students were to use a certain stairway and not enter the elementary part of the school. One large senior boy ignored the rules routinely and stomped past, walking as loudly as he could in cowboy boots. He deliberately used the wrong stairs. He had been in chemical dependency treatment, had a less-than-pleasant home situation, and most teachers hated to hassle or cross him up over anything that was not of major importance--partly because of retaliation and partly because he was having a difficult period in his life. I finally engaged in casual conversation in the hall with him about nonschool subjects, and soon he was using the right stairs--apparently no longer caring to defy me.

Incident #20

This fourth grade student seemed to thrive on negative behaviors with peers. He compulsively sucked on things in his mouth (especially his thick, red shoe laces from hiking boots) which repulsed everyone. A persistent tattler, he would tattle about everything and anything, much of which was made up. He frequently picked his nose and ate the contents, which was a great source of ridicule. He would come to school with tall tales that were obviously false, even to fourth graders, such as making $200 babysitting in an evening (when he never babysat at all), and his dad drove his truck around the world last weekend. These stories continued to damage his credibility. The more he tattled, cried, and fibbed, the more the other children wanted to tease and torment him because of the reaction they would get. This is as though it were a self-fulfilling prophecy, since he brought on the problems and conflicts himself. How can this vicious cycle be stopped?

These are just a few ideas. Some would be productive to use, some would not. The most stimulating situations to role play are those generated by yourself and your class.

Keep in mind that role playing can be used with colleagues and by you as a teacher with your students. Role playing ways to react to incidents with feedback can be a powerful way to test yourself in a safe situation.

CHAPTER XV

A FINAL WORD FOR EDUCATORS

The United States has been given no guarantee of survival, and without your help, it may not. So, please don't allow uncaring students, unsupportive taxpayers, and negative tirades weaken your resolve. Your job is and will continue to be our country's most important.

Our founding fathers were also concerned with survival, and it is in this sense I'm using the term. I'm talking about subtle changes taking place. About how our country is becoming an unpleasant place to live. About how grandparents cannot take grandchildren to ballgames without exposing them to abrasive and profane language; how police officers cannot break up disputes without risking physical retaliation; how campers cannot leave equipment unattended; and about old women who get attacked just because some get pleasure from beating them up.

Our country is being taken over by those who neither care nor understand anyone's rights but their own. That's why you are important. Now, more than ever.

Our country needs your guidance, your courage, and your stability. Many Americans have come to believe that blaring stereos, insults (verbal and nonverbal), and vulgarities are just the price for living in an affordable home near available employment. Well, it is not, and you can do something about it.

You have access to future judges, policepersons, newscasters, senators, film producers, and editors. You interact with every soon-to-be influential person in our country.

Society has entrusted you with discovering, teaching, and enforcing the standards necessary for a civilized society to survive. That is your charge, that is your responsibility.

You know what's appropriate and what isn't; what society can tolerate and what it cannot; which behaviors are normal and which won't be outgrown; which cruel actions are deliberate and which are just thoughtless--trust your feelings and act on them. Your assessment of a student's behavior is still the most significant long-range predictor for determining whether a student will adjust socially or become delinquent.

No one has the right to interfere with another's right to learn--other parents of children have rights, too. And no one has the right to deliberately hurt and harass another, for no one deserves to live in fear.

These truths you can still believe. And you can also still believe that you don't do a child a favor by allowing him or her to behave so obnoxiously that he or she alienates you and everyone else around them. Condoning this sort of behavior is the antithesis of being humane, emphatic, and compassionate.

As an educator, you must care enough for students to teach them the responsibilities that come with living in a democratic society; as an educator, you must love students enough to teach them the meaning of freedom; and as an educator, you must teach your students that the survival of a quality life in America still rests upon the foundations of decency, civility, and manners.

Find solace in the fact that you know you are important; in the fact that you really do know what needs to be done and how to do it.

APPENDIX A

QUESTIONS FOR DISCUSSION

1. How might you increase your students' stake in conformity?

2. How might you, specifically, prove to yourself that a student is behaving as best he/she is capable of behaving?

3. How do you show respect for your class?

4. If you sent the "I" message: "I am unable to teach when it is so noisy," and a student or students said, "So, quit; you're not that great, anyway," how might you react?

5. How are children the same today as they were two generations ago?

6. How do you distinguish between unintentional misconduct and willful disobedience?

7. What do you like about the grade level of students you teach?

8. What might you say in defense of the statement, "Discipline is the most important subject we teach"?

9. What did you learn about discipline the first year on the job you didn't know before?

10. How do you minimize the attention given to students who nearly monopolize your time?

11. How important are board members, superintendents, and principals in the realm of discipline?

12. What are the aims of punishment?

13. Is it essential for a teacher to like all of her students? Can a teacher be an effective teacher if he dislikes one or more of his students?

14. Why do we make rules that are not enforceable?

15. Classroom pride--is it a good or bad thing?

16. Does being organized ease discipline problems? Can there be too much organization?

17. How effective is time out (removal from class)? Do you feel it is an effective discipline tool?

18. How has the role of the parent changed the role of the teacher and school in disciplining the student?

19. What is the main reason teachers fail in discipline?

20. How far should we go and how much should we sacrifice other children to teach the chronically disruptive child?

21. How do you feel about the comment: "To make the students respect you, do not smile until after Thanksgiving"?

22. Why do some discipline programs work for some teachers and not for others?

23. What do you do about constant "nit-picking" among the staff when the administrator does nothing to rectify the problem?

24. Do I have a moral obligation to expect the best from all my students? It is _their_ life, you know.

25. How do you keep control of a big group (over 50) when you are rehearsing for a musical/play?

26. How can you begin to like a student that presently you don't like?

27. You have apparently lost control with a class in reference to classroom discipline. What can you do to re-establish acceptable classroom discipline without losing self-respect?

28. How does one determine "fair punishment" for the offense committed by a student?

29. Do some teachers actually have personalities and styles that promote discipline problems? If so, can these people be worked with to correct their problem area to become more effective teachers?

30. What model of discipline presented in this book and what attitude presented best match your personality and style? Why?

CRITICAL INCIDENTS

1. I had only been teaching for a few days when I was confronted with "organized trouble." The eighth grade class was a difficult class to manage. They liked to goof off and have "fun" rather than study or work. Their first organized prank was after they were all seated and the bell had rung; in unison, they counted 1, 2, 3, and then dropped their books on the floor. Since they all participated, it was hard to know how to deal with the incident. They also pulled stunts like passing their neighbor's books on to the next person down the line, and when they got to the row next to the windows, the books were then pushed outside through the window. Since they were so organized, I couldn't pick out one or two troublemakers.

2. I remember a seventh grade student I had several years ago who lied frequently. His mother was overly concerned about Dan's success in school. Success to this parent meant As and Bs. The student was an average student. The mother helped Dan with homework often, sometimes doing it for him, not merely telling him the answers, but actually doing the assignment herself. An incident developed when an assignment had been corrected in class and I happened to be moving around the room and I noticed the handwriting was not Dan's. When confronted, he said he did it himself--repeatedly. The incident was reported to the principal. Of course, the student lied to him, also. The parent called me and asked for a conference. Dan came with his mother and the three of us met for a conference. During what I thought was a productive discussion, Dan suddenly blurts out, yelling at the top of his voice, what a mean teacher I am; how much he hates me over and over again; how he hates my class; what a liar I am, etc. The mother just sat there with a smug look on her face. Needless to say, I felt devastated and did not know what I had done to deserve this. This was a new experience for me. The conference ended on a very sour note. I did not know how to handle the situation, and I am not sure I still do. What would you have done? Dan is now a freshman, and I have heard of incidents where other teachers have discovered assignments done by "Mommy."

3. During math class, a student was complaining about doing his work. He said he hated math and then

started to swear to express his disgust further. When I asked him to stop talking and get back to work, he told me I couldn't make him work, and if I tried, his dad would come to school and shoot me. His dad did show up the next day, but merely talked to the principal and me.

4. I was assigned to oversee a student lounge type of situation with anywhere from 50 to 150 juniors and seniors, many of whom I did not know. They were allowed much freedom, with one rule--no card playing. I was one of the few teachers who tried to enforce the rule. They reacted by making me their entertainment for that hour. The card players threw pennies at me if I turned my back, and even went so far as to blow up a bag of firecrackers in a bookcase. The principal wanted to know what I was doing to antagonize them, since "other teachers didn't have any trouble."

5. The wife of a friend of mine graduated from high school with honors. She then went to college and again graduated with honors and a degree in English. She got a job in a small town and began her career in education. She had never had any trouble with school or learning, so she could not relate to the problems her students were having. The kids became disruptive in class. They seemed to organize. They would drop books on the floor, many at the same time. At the end of the class period, they would all sit up rigid, stand, and slam desks. Then, as if on command, they would turn and march out of the room. Things of this nature continued for half the school year; she finally lost out to a nervous breakdown, and never taught again.

6. In terms of discipline, I thought and thought and nothing really significant came to mind. I decided to write about a situation that really bothered me the first year I was teaching. I was so idealistic and believed that I really could save those troubled students. I latched on to a student in one of my ninth grade social studies classes. He was a very troubled boy--anti-social, hard to relate to, family problems . . . it went on and on. I tried to relate to him, be nice to him, give him advice (none of this solicited), etc. In my fantasy world, I thought I was saving a potential juvenile delinquent from ruination! I was mortally wounded when he dropped out of school, and later I heard he had been in and out of jail with a criminal record. I have since put it all in

perspective. I still try to help kids--I've been a counselor now for eight years. I'm just more realistic! And I don't take things so personally.

7. While on a field trip, a tainted individual approached my class in the Minneapolis Public Library. I found out later he spoke to some of them in a dirty manner. I found out about it the next day, with many parents being upset.

8. As the students were gathering for an assembly, several sophomore boys lingered behind in a huddle near a low wall. The preschool children were at recess nearby. When everyone finally was in the auditorium, I returned to the wall to find out the reason for this activity. I found a lighted cigarette being used as the time-delay for setting off a cherry bomb. Had it been discovered by the preschool children instead of me, they easily could have been injured when it went off. As it was, I dismantled it and never made any comment about it to anyone. The mischief-makers were not given any attention, and were baffled as to what had happened.

9. I was observing during college in an inner-city art class. My first impression was the room looked organized, the students didn't, and the teacher seemed somewhat apathetic to it all. As I continued to observe, I wasn't sure when the class had actually begun, as the teacher could only manage to get a small group of the class's attention. She was talking very loudly, with little expression, for her instructions to be heard. As she went into her small supply closet to get the assignment paper, a student turned off the light, closed the door behind her, and did something to the lock to keep her in there. I felt helpless. As this was happening, students were now hanging out the windows, throwing art supplies around, and playing around her desk. What could I have done? Before I reached the closet, another student opened the door for her. I expected her to be furious, but instead was unconcerned and made a comment referring to she'd been meaning to get that lock fixed, and continued on with the lesson.

10. I had a student who would have temper tantrums. He was diabetic and his diet would affect his behavior; however, I do not feel that this was the entire cause of his tantrums. His temper would flare up very suddenly and sometimes for no apparent reason.

He would begin hitting and kicking his classmates. He was one of the bigger kids in the class, and I was afraid he would hurt someone. One day he took his arm and wiped off everything on the top of my desk. He would run out of the room and lock himself in the janitor's room or climb to the top of the monkey bars and refuse to come down. He sometimes would threaten to hurt himself, for example, jump off the monkey bars.

11. One day I had two senior boys put up the screen on a window and go out the window. I turned around and saw they were gone. The next thing I heard someone running on the roof.

12. What would you do to a first grader who filled his pants about three times a week, but would never report it? If I smelled him, I would send him to the nurse's office to change. He was referred to the Child Study Committee, checked out physically by the doctors, and parents were consulted weekly. Nothing seemed to change the behavior, and the child did not care at all about the problem. No person, though, could ever help him change or clean up. The principal's suggestion was to expel him.

13. A student showed up for class drunk and in a foul mood. When I confronted him about this, he took a swing at me. This happened in my first two weeks of teaching.

14. I had a boy in class who had a reputation for being a troublemaker, but I never had any trouble with him. One day, in the middle of class, he pulled quite a large knife out and started playing with it. I asked him to put it away "very politely." He said, "Why?" I replied because I didn't like it and, thank goodness, he put it away.

15. After I graduated from college, I taught second grade in a public school. Then I married. I so called "retired." After two years, I was approached and asked to finish teaching third grade in a parochial school. I did. The following year, I taught third grade in the other parochial school as a long-term sub. Then the two parochial schools combined. I applied for my old position as a third grade teacher. I was turned down. After pursuing the reasons, I was told that there was a faction of people who didn't like me because I was too "strict." After thinking this through, I asked to go before the school board and

explain my position. I simply told them that I came not begging for a job, but to make people aware of the situation I walked into the first year I subbed. I told them that the first day I walked into the class, a picture was drawn of me with the words "she is a pig." Then I proceeded to explain some of the many other disgraceful and undisciplined things done. I also explained that no parents approached me during the year so I could explain my side of it. I felt that the small group of people were judging me unfairly! The only thing I expected from the third graders was order and respect. That I accomplished by the end of the year. AMEN! The day following my board meeting, I was offered a contract. After that first year of teaching, my principal nominated me teacher of the year. P.S. I'm still teaching third grade today!

16. The kindergarten in which I teach is located in our senior high school, and my children must use the senior high bathroom facilities. Being a female teacher, I hesitate entering the boys' bathroom, especially in a high school. But, one day I felt it necessary. I was waiting in the hallway outside the bathrooms and, as the children finished, they came out and lined up. I could hear noise from the boys' bathroom and then a piercing scream. I opened the door and started in and ran into a high school student who started shouting at me about "keeping my _____ _____ _____ nose out of the boys' can." As it turned out, one of the boys had turned out the lights, causing the scream, so no one was hurt, but, I didn't know that at the time; so, should I have gone in or not?

17. On my first day of teaching--first hour of the day--I entered the room and found a senior boy standing on my desk.

18. I had a 10-year-old girl who would never read directions on her own. I really believed that she was emotionally disturbed to the point of needing professional help; but, I was teaching at a small private school which made no provisions for such students. The girl's parents refused to believe that she had a problem. Even after I had given directions to the class, she would whine, whimper, curse, and threaten--saying that she didn't understand and needed me to come to her desk. So, one day I gave her a sheet of math problems that I was reasonably sure she knew how to do, and then casually told her that I wouldn't help her and she would stay at her desk until she was

finished. She sat at her desk and cried and cried. She said she "forgot how to divide." She said that her mother (who was the director of the school, incidentally) would hire a new teacher. She said that her parents didn't like for her to be "frustrated." She said that if I would "just help her a little," she could do the math. She stomped her feet and swore at me.

19. The course I teach is auto mechanics, and it is an elective for 11th and 12th grade students. Due to the fact that it is a high-interest course, plus being an elective, I haven't had many "incidents" in the classroom. Also, I'm one of the stricter teachers and also tend to produce a skilled person in my field; therefore, I think most kids react differently in my classroom than they might in others. The two incidents I will write about happened during lunch supervision this year.

A group of ninth graders were sitting at a table, and, as they started to leave, a fellow supervisor noticed some food articles left behind. She stopped one of the kids and asked him to take them to the trash can. He refused. I noticed them talking and went over and told the boy that he was to pick up after lunch for arguing with the lady. He refused initially, but then said he would. At the end of lunch, I looked around and he had skipped out. The next day, I took him over to the principal at lunchtime and told him the story, and he backed me up and assigned two days of cleanup. The boy did the cleanup and the problem seemed over.

The second incident occurred about a week after the first. I was standing in the lunchroom and a young boy walked up to me and looked me in the eye, much like he was going to ask a question, and said, "I hate you." I was shocked. I had never had him in class, never had any dealings with him, never disciplined him or anything. I said, "What?" He repeated it. I asked him why he said that since we had never had a conflict. He refused to comment and simply repeated his line. I took him to the assistant principal and told him to repeat what he said to me. He did, and the principal was surprised. Eventually, I found out that he was a good friend of the boy in the first incident and was standing up for his buddy. The next day, he came up to me and apologized.

20. The following incident has occurred off but

102

mostly on during the entire school year. This is
behavior observed by several parents (of the young
children) at the bus stop of a large apartment complex
in a Midwest metro area city. The children involved
range from K through 6 grades--approximately two to
three in each grade. The sixth grader, Derek, and a
fifth grader, Byron, alternate being the bully and boss
of all the other children. They have more rules than
you can count, and these are added to continually suit
their needs. They require books and schoolbags to be
put in a specific order each day. The youngest
children are all to be last on the bus every day. The
older kids make fun of the younger ones' clothes or
things they say, and sometimes call them names and
swear at them. The young children even hate riding the
bus because they have become so intimidated and afraid.
No one really knew who could do anything about this
problem--some of the parents tried, with no success.
Could we have involved the school principal?

21. Ricky is in my kindergarten class. His
problems are shown in his behavior and lack of respect
for my authority. He does not follow any directions
given. He will not be seated with the class in any
activity, but wanders about or does what he wants to.
I usually have to physically sit him down, which has
resulted in screaming, kicking, and throwing things.
Ricky pouts continually about something all day. In
any seatwork or independent work, he demands my
constant assistance. When he does not get that
assistance immediately, he again pouts, throws things,
and makes threats--"I hate you" and "I don't like you."
(He was one of my favorite, most likable children I've
taught by the end of the year.)

22. I had a third grade boy who is very quiet and
doesn't share much in class. We were talking about
animals in science, and he raised his hand. I was so
excited, I called on him immediately. He said he was
riding around with his uncle last night and they saw a
cow. I asked him what kind of cow it was, and he said
it was a fuckin' dead cow!!

23. During my second month of teaching, I was
invited to a masquerade party at the home of a second
grade teacher at the local Catholic school. At this
time, this woman was basically my only friend in town.
Early in the evening, four of my high school students
entered the house and were served beer by someone who
didn't realize their age (they were in costume). The

students drank the beer in my presence (they were less than 10 feet from me). I was thankful that I was drinking Diet Pepsi! At the time, I didn't realize that I had no choice but to report it to the principal. The students were all members of the choir and were to be excluded from participation in the following two concerts. Needless to say, the students were very upset with me for "ratting" on them; but, I was taken by surprise when my friend, the second grade teacher, asked me to come over to her house on Monday evening and then told me that she wanted me to go to the principal and take back what I had said. She wanted me to change my story and tell the principal that the students had only been holding the beer, not drinking it. She was worried that her job would be in jeopardy because minors had been served liquor in her house. I did not take back my story, and our friendship suffered because of it.

24. In mid-January on a Saturday when the wind chill was near -90°, I took a group of students out at 7:00 a.m. to attend the one-act play contest in a town about 20 miles away. When we got there, we realized that we were the first ones there. Upon entering the dark school, it became clear to us that there was to be no contest that day. Because of a scheduling mix-up, I had mistakenly taken my students to the contest ONE WEEK EARLY! It was the most embarrassing experience of my life.

25. On the way to phy. ed. class, going to the field--boys and girls had phy. ed. at the same time, but classes separate (the field was two blocks away form school)--three boys decided to play a practical joke on a girl. As she was going up the hill, one boy ran up behind her, reached for her gym shorts, and pulled them down.

26. An elementary teacher in my home town had a very "hard to control" class. There was one boy who instigated most of the trouble, and had his own little following. The teacher had tried every type of discipline, to no avail. She had also asked the principal for help, but got no aid there, either. To make a long story short, she made a threat that she had to follow through on. She threatened to put animal manure on their noses if they didn't behave. They didn't, so she had to. The incident got attention from all local papers, and also national news--quite an event for a small town in Iowa! The teacher was known

by her students as a "good" teacher. She was asked to leave that school. A "good" teacher?

27. The last hour study hall teacher was tired of students abusing hall passes. One such abuse was to get a pass for the bathroom and cut out of school 10 to 15 minutes early. So, his new policy was for no more passes to be issued the last 15 minutes of study hall. All students abided by the new policy, except one. He took exception to the policy, claiming that it was a personal attack on him because the teacher didn't like him. So, being a "Golden Glover," he squared off and punched the teacher in the nose, causing his glasses to fly clear across the room. The other students started cheering him on. Two black eyes, a broken nose, and several missing teeth later, the student got a pass, forged the teacher's name, and left. The next day, the student was in school, while the teacher never did come back, and left the profession right after the fight.

28. One of my students spit in another's food at lunch.

29. In my first year of teaching, I left my purse in my desk while going out into the hall. When I came back, I saw a high school boy come out of my room. In checking my purse, a $10.00 bill was gone. I reported this to the superintendent, but no action was taken. How could I have confronted the intruder?

30. John was a student that up through grade four was diagnosed as mentally retarded and was allowed total freedom in very small classroom situations. When I obtained him in grade five, he did not want to be told what to do. He did many things that could upset a teacher or a classroom. Examples of the things he did:

A. One time he took his glasses off and jumped up and down on them, smashing them. He did this because I told him to eat his lunch that was packed for him.

B. Some boys flushed his head in a urinal because of his teasing and nagging.

C. Stamped on a full carton of milk, splattering milk all over. Why? He responded, "Just to see what would happen."

D. Hid in a locker, causing three teachers a

lot of grief looking for him for an hour.

E. Threw his lunch pail at a student. The student ducked, and it went through a large double-pane window.

I managed to discover that John was not mentally retarded. In fact, he could read extremely fast and had very good comprehension. In the area of reading, he was very gifted. The trouble was he read so fast out loud that you could not understand him. I managed to get him to slow down. When he found out that he could get positive feedback on his school work, the incidents began to be fewer. His grandmother and grandfather were so pleased that he was not retarded that they became more positive with him at home. He was staying with his grandparents because his dad was in the Navy and his mother had to be institutionalized because of a nervous breakdown.

31. Every once in awhile, I see some of my students smoking around town. Sometimes I've seen other students drinking who are under age. I ignore these situations rather than get involved. How far should teachers carry over with their discipline?

32. Dad always walks Kelly to school. He also picks her up at the end of the day. He restricts her activities with her other third grade friends. She tells us he sleeps with her and keeps the bedroom door locked "so her brothers won't come in and bother her."

33. In the beginning of the year, a boy who was repeating kindergarten was controlling his parents and me by insisting that he did not want to come to school. He did this through temper tantrums, both at home and at school. He refused to ride the school bus; his parents brought him in from his country home every school day. When his dad would bring him to the room, he would kick, scream, and cling to his father's legs. One particularly bad day, he left the school with his coat and schoolbag, unbeknownst to me, of course! He was found at his grandmother's and was immediately returned to school under severe protest. Time and stubbornness worked out this problem.

34. The following incident occurred during my second year of teaching. The class was a self-contained group of third graders. Sharon's mother was a very intense person, one who involved herself in

things to a degree of overbearance. She would even go so far as to keep files on all information that was processed through the school district. She would also make verbal complaints criticizing community activities, whether or not the activities took place in her own area. Sharon had difficulty learning a specific math concept. She took home an assignment paper that had more incorrect answers than correct ones. It was the first time the concept was presented. Sharon's mother reacted to this bad paper by calling each parent in my class. She asked each in turn if their child was having difficulty in math. She also implied that I was too young and inexperienced to be teaching. She believed me to be about 17 years old. I first learned about these phone calls from my principal, who had been informed by a concerned parent who did not approve of the way in which Mrs. D. was handling the matter. He was very supportive of me and said that he would back me 100%. Mrs. D. had never confronted me to discuss Sharon's difficulty in math. In fact, she made very effort to be pleasant and seemingly supportive of me whenever we did meet. The immediate problem of the phone calling was never officially resolved, although as Sharon's math grades improved, her mother's attitude seemingly improved, as well. Sharon's mother and I never openly discussed her actions. The most that was said was spoken to me at the end of the school year, when she congratulated me on a job well done and said that she had never meant to cause trouble.

35. I was called into the principal's office and was told a parent was upset because I used the student's nickname in class. He wouldn't tell me the name of the student or the parents, so I walked out on the conversation. There were so many nicknames in the class and I felt it was my right to know the people involved so I could refrain from hurting the student. Should I have done anything else?

36. I had just walked into the classroom and I caught my seventh grade student strangling another student. I stepped on my student's foot and pulled him back from the young man. He turned around and hit me in the stomach (I was six months pregnant). Another teacher who had come into the room saw the problem and helped me to get my student to his desk. The student grabbed the desk and was determined to just sit and swear at us. I rang the intercom for help, and the principal and assistant principal came. They first

talked to the student to remove him from the room. He would not remove his hands from the desk. They forcibly removed his hands and carried him from the classroom. The principals and myself took him to a quiet room and tried talking to him. He was swearing and calling me names. He finally said he was going to kill us all. The principals decided to take him home. Upon reaching his house, he ran into the house and grabbed a gun and told them he was going to shoot. The gun was a BB gun, but no one knew this. The student was later sent to a boys' ranch in Minnesota. The sad part of this is the administrators wanted to bring this student back into the school after a period of two weeks. The other teacher and myself had to write a grievance to keep this from happening. We won our case, but the real problem we learned later was that the administration did not want to pay the fees to get this child help in a boys' ranch, but felt it would be cheaper to keep the student in the school system.

37. This happened in a first grade classroom. A child of mine had severe temper tantrums. He always had to be the center of things, the leader, the winner in a phy. ed. game, to do things the way he wanted to do them. This would range from reading the story in reading class that he wanted to read, to winning a game involving math flash cards, to being the person who never gets caught in tag. When he didn't accomplish this, he would cry in a very loud voice, stomp his feet, and hit his head on the floor or a wall. This eventually led to the point where he chased an aide around the room with a scissors because she wouldn't let him do what he wanted to. In addition, he started to move objects around--like my file cabinet, his chair and desk. This was the worst he got. After being seen by the school psychologist, he was committed to the University of Minnesota hospital for psychological health.

38. During my second year of teaching, I had a fifth grade boy who had been having all sorts of problems with other students, teachers, parents, etc. At the end of the day as students were getting ready to go home, I noticed glue dripping from his desk. Examining his desk, I found he had spread glue all over his desk, and not only that, but had glued all of the books on the classroom bookshelf.

39. Once a junior high boy let the air out of my tires. When the father was called in, he said the boy

had to pump up only one of the tires, as other boys had also participated.

40. A third grade boy asked to go to the bathroom about five minutes after bathroom break. I told him that he would have to wait. After class, he headed for the bathroom, had an accident on the way, became embarrassed, and headed for home and not for his homeroom. He walked three miles without his coat in winter. We did not notice he was gone until an hour later, when his angry mother called.

41. I had detention duty, which was in an area a bit secluded, away from the general hustle-and-bustle area. A boy pulled a knife out. There were, I believe, three boys in there, and one had a reputation of being a pretty "rough" kid. I was petrified. Very calmly and with as much strength as I could find inside me, I said, "This is not the place for that; put it away, or it will be mine." He did, and I said thank you under my breath.

42. While showing a film to my eighth grade science class, I noticed Mike, sitting at the back of the class, seemed very preoccupied. I worked my way slowly to where he was sitting and saw that he was masturbating. After I had recovered from my surprise, I told him to put his "toy" away. I didn't make an issue of it, nor did I mention it again. What would you have done?

43. As a first-year teacher, I had an experience that rally snowballed out of hand. The students were reading a story on the origin of the game Monopoly. A student asked me if we could take a day and play Monopoly. I said no. Another student told me all the other classes get to play Monopoly. I told them maybe they should join the other class. (Mistake number one) The next day, only half of my class showed up on time. Rather than having a sense of humor about them trying to get into another class, I sent them to the office to get a pass for being late to class. The office wrote them all passes for the numerous excuses. I sent them back to the office to explain the real reason they were late.

44. At this time, mid-term reports had been sent home. One purpose is to notify parents that their child had poor or failing grades. This boy had received his, and on it I had recorded low test scores,

poor daily work, and missing assignments. The report indicated that the student was failing the class. Also, another important thing to know, he needed this credit to graduate. When the class period was to begin, I was standing in the back of the room. He came storming into the room, looked around for me, focused in on me, and started yelling and screaming at me about his mid-term report. He was calling me and the class names; he was totally out of control. I approached him and asked him to leave immediately, and we would discuss this at another time. As he left, the door slammed shut so hard I thought that the glass would break. At a later time, we discussed his grades, where he needed to improve. He also apologized for his behavior and was going to try and be more conscious of his class work.

45. At a conference with a parent of an "active" first grader, the father said flatly that he has a belt "this wide" (and measured about three inches on his fingers) that he uses on his son at home. I had been offered the belt to keep on the corner of my desk and had permission to use it. I told him quickly that I didn't think that was at all necessary and changed the subject. But, as teachers, we have an obligation to report "child abuse" if witnessed or strongly suspected. Was this abuse? In my book--yes. But, I let it go. Twelve years later and I'm still wondering about this boy; how did he grow up having been beaten as a first grader with a three-inch belt?

46. During a potty patrol, Kathy was discovered smoking in the girls' lavatory. She denied this when in the parent-principal conference, and also when the teacher who caught her was brought in on the conference. The parents' comment to the teacher was--"I have to believe one of you and, since I know my daughter, I have to believe her."

47. We have a fifth grade teacher in our building who has a special way of dealing with his discipline problems--he opens his door and lets the student out into the hall. Our music teacher, who moves from classroom to classroom, counted the number of times she had seen one particular student in the hall one day. She saw him between every activity. The students are disturbing other classes, other students in the halls, and people working in the office. How do you tell a teacher of 10 years that he should keep his students in his room and teach them something? The principal

doesn't do anything about it!

48. I had a student literally take a desk apart in the back of the classroom. He took out the screws and pulled the top off. I didn't know how to handle this situation. The whole class was laughing and giving him reinforcement.

49. In my second year of teaching, I sent home unsatisfactory reports at nine weeks as required by the administration. I had a student's mother call me before school after receiving the report. She read me the riot act like you wouldn't believe. Needless to say, I lost my temper, etc. It ruined my day. I was so upset about losing my temper! I later found out that she did that periodically to teachers and was mentally ill.

50. While the entire staff was attending a preschool faculty meeting, an argument began on the third floor. The faculty meeting was on the first floor at the opposite end of the school complex. A sixth grade boy who tends to irritate and antagonize took on a very strong eighth grade boy with a short temper. Pushing and shoving led to a slugfest with much bleeding from noses. The younger boy was pushed up against the stair railing, which could have led to a three-flight fall. The younger boy ran from the building and sat in a snowbank. Other students ran to the office and reported to the secretary. About this time, the faculty were reporting to their classrooms. The principal expelled both boys for the usual three days. We continue to have preschool faculty meetings which run overtime, past the time teachers are normally in the rooms and halls.

51. I was teaching Spanish to a group of elementary students during summer school. One particular student in the class complained that she was not learning, nor enjoying, the class. She was given the option to transfer to another class, but refused. Towards the end of summer school, she entered the classroom one morning carrying a tape recorder with a note addressed to me. The note informed me that the parents wanted to tape my lesson so they could find out exactly what I was teaching my students. I took the note and recorder from the student and asked her to take her seat. After giving the class an assignment, I went down to the principal's office and handed him the note and recorder. How would you have handled this

situation?

52. As I was approaching the girls' locker room, I found a boy (whom I did not know) coming out of the locker room. (There were three classes of girls in there dressing and showering.) When I asked him what he was doing in there, he spit on me and started running up the stairs. As I followed him, he spit on me again, so I started chasing him down the hall. When he ran outside, I decided I wasn't going to go any further. As I went to the office to report the incident, he went across the street and raped an elderly lady while holding a knife to her throat. He was apprehended a short time later. Because he assaulted a teacher (spitting on me), I was called to court where he was sentenced to Red Wing--mainly because of his assault on the other lady.

53. When Daniel first came to kindergarten, he did not speak a word for the first three days. He refused to do simple tasks. He simply shook his head no. When he finally did utter some words, they were, "I can't." He obviously needed his self-confidence boosted, and he really needed some love. However, Daniel was very large and hefty for his age; he was dirty and he smelled very strong of urine. Some days his pants were thoroughly wet. Reaching out and helping Daniel was to be a real challenge. I couldn't even get him to smile! After a lot of time and patience, Daniel finally gained enough confidence to at least try a task. I found that I could hug him and love him. (Sometimes the hugs were short, because you had to hold your breath.) The first big breakthrough was when he could finally skip (after three-fourths of a year of practice). From there, he found that he was capable and could perform tasks. After a while, school work improved and even a bit of personality started to bloom.

54. A couple of years ago, while I was (as usual) junior class moderator, I was chaperoning a prom. Early in the evening, while students were still arriving, I went to my car to retrieve something that was needed at the dance. As I headed back to the door, I saw a student arriving with his date, skylined by the horizon, tipping up a flask. I was extremely upset, and reacted without thoughts about consequences. I walked right up close to the student, told him to get rid of the bottle, which was obviously liquor from the smell on him, turned, and went into

112

the hall. The student came in shortly after and was subdued for the rest of the evening, which went well. Only later did I realize the consequences of my action. The student was the number one golfer on a team perennially in contention for the state title. His father is a lawyer, and in a similar incident related to athletic eligibility, had caused quite a row. I reported the incident, however, and was surprised to get absolutely no feedback. The student did not play in the state meet, where our team lost the title by one stroke.

55. One of my main problems concerns a co-worker. When I am in my office during prep hour, lunch, etc., she stands in the hall talking to other teachers, or uses the phone, or goes to the office. Her students are left unsupervised and may be operating sewing machines, ranges, or, in other words, could cause injury to themselves or others. I don't feel it's my job to supervise her students or to answer their questions about how to do something, or specifically answer their questions as to where she is. My main worry is, "How liable am I for injuries or damages when she is not in her room?" Sometimes she lets students from study hall work in the clothing lab while she has another class in the foods room. Once my block participant assisted removing a machine needle from a student's finger while "teacher" was out. The principal has been informed of the above situation and supposedly spoke to her. The mania still exists. What to do?

56. Sometimes the "little" or "gray" area of discipline can be perplexing as to what is the correct reaction. Example: I have an office adjacent to my classroom that can be locked. One evening I had a meeting, and after leaving my coat in the office, I forgot to lock it. When I returned, walked in, and turned on the lights, I found a boy and a girl embracing passionately in the office. I was upset that they were in the office, but so surprised I was speechless. What would be the proper reaction?

57. On the first day of school in 1984, a handsome boy, his good-looking mother, and our principal walked into my classroom. I welcomed them and showed Danny a seat, etc., and soon his mother left. Our principal whispered, "I'll need to help you." Soon, I knew the reason for the whispered words. Although Danny was intelligent, his academic

performance in reading was poor, but other subjects were O.K., and his "sex" vocabulary was amazing for a first grader; so was his language relating to sex. "Pinching the buns;" kissing and chasing girls; exclaiming, "My, what sexy legs!"; and pointing to their "tits" (as he called them) were his sex offenses. His attention span was short; his desk and belongings were almost always a mess. He was constantly "on the move." He loved to fight with boys on the playground. (He said his divorced dad was a wrestler.) He would throw things when he was angry. Many times I had to send home his mom's belongings like lipstick, lip ice, chapstick, credit card, Blue Shield card, playing cards, etc., with his third grade sister. One day he came to school with "black marker" dots and marks all over his face and both of his arms. He looked terrible, so I made him clean his face and arms. The janitor caught him trying to make the fire alarm go off. He turned on the outside of the school's water faucet and sent a big stream of water rushing down the sidewalk. Luckily I saw him doing it. (Perhaps he was just curious and didn't know how to turn off the water. This was his explanation). When I'd reprimanded him according to our assertive discipline plan, he'd whisper, or mutter, or speak out, "Shut up," or, "I do not have to do what you tell me!" And one day when he was in an angry mood, he scratched me on the arm. I did not keep track of the times he was in the principal's office for violation of our rules, nor the times teachers and I spent conferring with his mother and him. Our school tried to help him and his mother during the seven months he was here. The last day of school for Danny was May 8, 1987, and a few weeks later we received notice that he enrolled elsewhere. At this time, my principal said, "One thing I know and have learned about Danny, and that is--he has learned to survive!" Note: This boy was one out of the many students I have had like this in 30 years of teaching.

58. This incident happened my third year of teaching and shows how you really have to watch everything you say. During a journalism lecture, I noticed Mike, a 12th grader, not taking notes as usual. The next morning at 8:00, he came in and said he didn't understand the day's assignment. I said, "If you use your notes from yesterday, you can do the worksheet easily." "I don't have my notes anymore; I lost them," explained Mike. "You mean, you never took them," I retorted. At this point, he started

laughing. "Well," I said, "you had better find some notes. As for me, right now I'm going to the lounge and get some coffee before class starts." When class started at 8:15, I noticed Mike wasn't there. I thought to myself that he was probably skipping since his work wasn't done. At the end of class, a principal came to my room and said he had two very angry parents in his room who wondered why it was more important for me to have coffee than to help their kid. This kid had gone home and used my one statement against me to save his own butt. I was really angry and hurt that this kid would do this. I had to face these parents and try to explain what really happened. Although they cooled down considerably, I still think they were very skeptical of me, even after the explanation, as a teacher who was a "lounger." I felt angry and out of control in this situation because I did say this, but it was the kid who was at fault.

59. Between classes, I was leaving my room to go to the classroom next door. Just as I was about to exit, two eighth grade boys came running through the door--one chasing the other. It was so unexpected and happened so fast that I was unable to move before being literally knocked to the floor. I ended up with a cut lip, a lump on my head, and a bruised arm and shoulder. By the time I regained my composure, it was absolutely silent in my room--no easy feat for 28 eighth graders--and I am sure they were all afraid I was angry enough to do something violent! Instead, I asked them whoever was responsible for the accident to stop after class and talk to me. No one did. Two days later, one of the boys called me at home to apologize, because his parents had learned from their daughter of the incident. He told me who the other boy was. When confronted, the second boy denied being involved. The administration felt it best to not pursue the situation any further.

60. I had been working with Rebecca (third grader) every day for about two-thirds of the school year. She was rather moody and sometimes did not want to cooperate, but we had never really had too much of a problem. On the day of this incident, she was acting unusually upset and did not want to work. After I'd tried to get her to work and she would not, I very quietly asked her if she was doing her best and if something was bothering her. She started to kick and scream and throw things. I was able to get her classroom teacher, who tried also to settle her down.

She only got worse. We brought in the principal, but she only got more and more out of control. It was like she could not stop herself; she had so much anger to let out. She tried to break windows, run into the sreet, and throw anything she could find. This behavior continued until we were able to reach her mother and she could get to school. Later we discovered Rebecca was having many emotional problems, especially dealing with a younger sister who had her birthday the day of the blowup. Although I never had problems with Rebecca again, her classroom teacher did, as well as the music and phy. ed. teachers. It was a frightening and helpless feeling I hope never to go through again.

61.   I was in the gym with another fifth grade class and their male teacher. The students were playing a game and getting along fine, until Randy refused to play by the rules. Mr. M. told him he was "out" (part of the game), but Randy refused to go. Mr. M. took him by the arm to escort him off the floor. Randy jerked loose and started swinging. The fight finally ended with Randy being thrown up against a locker. Randy ran home (nine miles into the country), told his parents, and, one hour later, the parents were at school demanding to see Mr. M. and me. The parents obviously felt Randy had done no wrong. The father said, "I've always told my boys if they can't finish a fight, I'd finish it for them. The principal <u>refused</u> to sit in on this conference. He was of no help. We both came very close to being sued, and the administration wouldn't even discuss the situatin with Mr. M. and myself.

62.   I had a sixth grade boy in class who was receiving individual counseling at a clinic, plus was on medication for hyperactivity. However, his counselor/doctor kept adjusting his medication and his behavior was unpredictable from one day to the next, so the same approach used on him would sometimes produce very different results. One day, during discussion of students' ambitions for the future, he shouted out, "I want to be an arsonist." I ignored him. A few minutes later, he shouted out, "I want to die in a whorehouse!" I separated him from the rest of the class, then sent a note to his parents, who had a history of being very supportive. They grounded him for two weeks, and he was sullen in class for that period of time.

63.   This past year, a retired teacher who did
substitute   teaching in our school   district filled in
for the band director who was absent. The kids didn't
take   their work   seriously for   this substitute.   He
belittled them by saying what a poor job they were
doing   and   how   he   was   entitled   to   criticize them
because of his vast musical background. This resulted
in the students really showing how "poorly" they could
perform   with   their   instruments.   The   substitute
teacher   walked out of the classroom before the end of
class,   entered the   teachers'   lounge, explained what
happened to anyone who would listen, said "good-bye,"
and   hasn't returned to   school as a   substitute ever
again.   The administration was told, "Don't ever call
me again."

64.   My first year of teaching I was a victim of
an infatuation by an older mentally retarded male
student.   This boy started out by collecting pictures
of pretty girls out of magazines.   His collection of
pictures   turned   into   infatuations   with   T.V. stars
(female),   then to a real-life female (me).   He
flirted, gave me gifts, and told me he loved me.   I
didn't take him seriously and did not know what else
he was doing.   A small notebook was found with my
name, address, and phone number in it. There was also
a   planned-out wedding with me, including names   for
groomsmen,   bridesmaids,   how   much   cake   to have,
champagne,   where to go for a honeymoon,   and the
wedding date. He was not a student of mine, but I was
told by his teacher to ignore him. What would this
boy   do if his actions were acknowledged by a girl?
Or, what would his next step be? (from pictures, to
T.V. stars, to real life, to?)

65.   Some   old   coins   from   a grandparent's
collection were passed around the room. One coin
disappeared.   Being upset, the teacher announced that
the   whole   class   must   stay   after school   until the
missing coin reappeared. At 3:25 p.m., the teacher
didn't know what to do. The guilty one either would
not or was too frightened to admit his guilt publicly;
mothers would be worrying. The teacher explained that
she   could not keep them any longer, although she knew
it wasn't fair to let the guilty one go scot-free.
She was sure he was sorry he took the coin.   Were
there any suggestions from the class?   One boy
suggested this idea. Have each student write a note.
If you did not take the coin, write "no" and sign your
name.   The one who took the coin could sign "yes" and

sign his name. The teacher said she would let the guilty person remain unknown that day and settle it later. It actually worked.

66. It was my second year of teaching. I had had a terrific first year with first graders who were now all second graders right across the hall. As the year progressed, I noticed a big change, particularly in their facial expressions, which had initially been filled with sunshine smiles. (Could this be "normal" attitude change in second grade?) Many faces were drawn, eyes at the ground when we passed in the hall or met at lunch. Then I witnessed something I'd never seen or never considering doing myself--the teacher grabbed one of the children, dragged him into the hall, slammed him up against a locker, and proceeded with verbal punishment. I soon found out that "that's the way it is with Mrs. _____" . . . my second year of teaching, so I didn't do a thing except cry about it when no one else was around. Who was I to rock her boat, a nearly retirement-age teacher? (I'm still angry and frustrated with myself for having turned away from the problem like everyone else did!)

67. It was my first day of substitute teaching in 12 years. My assignment was a fourth grade class that had been labeled a "bad group." Within the first five minutes, the "homeroom" class exchanged rooms. I was now faced with faces that were somewhat similar, and many which were totally new. After a rather exhausting day (many "planned" activities took five minutes rather than the 40 minutes allotted), I was faced with the last academic subject to present. New challenges were presented with yet another different group of faces. The class disruptor chose to test the waters. After refusing to begin the assignment, or to clear off his desk and to get the proper materials, I quietly asked the student to join me at the table to finish his work. He refused yet another time. I then approached the student "eyeball to eyeball" and in a whisper said, "Please come to the table now, and stop acting like such a jerk." The child screamed, "I'm not a jerk!" and ran out of the room. I placed a student in charge and quickly fled after the student, finding him in the bathroom. Standing by the bathroom door, I apologized for my anger and told the student I should not have called him a jerk. He indicated I had hurt his feelings. I countered with, "Yes, I'm sure I did, and I apologize for that, as well." We returned to the classroom and order was restored. After the

school day had ended, I approached a fellow teacher, repeated the incident and sequence of events, and asked for the child's home telephone number. I called the student's parents, apologized once again, and was thanked by the mother for calling. Then I hung up the phone and cried. How else could this situation have been avoided (other than NOT calling the child a jerk)? Did I overreact by calling parents?

68. I began teaching third grade in the middle of the school year. The teacher that I replaced quit because of the tough group of kids and personal problems. Of course, I wasn't told this when I was hired. In addition to this tough group, I had to contend with Jimmy, who was severely disturbed. Daily he disrupted my class. One day he was completely out of control--running across the tops of desks yelling profanities. I sent another student to summon the principal (who had a short time to retirement and didn't want any problems). The principal came to my door. Jimmy took my large dictionary and threw it at him. It barely missed him. Red-faced, he turned and walked out of he room. I got the message--handle it yourself. I was shocked and angry. What should I have done?

69. I had a problem with a first grader this year who always felt a need to play with himself. I discussed this problem with his parents, but when I found no results, I decided to talk to him myself. I explained how this is a very private thing (avoiding any moralistic conflicts), and that he could not continue this behavior. After our talk, he felt the need to go to the bathroom quite often, but he didn't play with himself anymore in the classroom.

70. I have a girl in my first grade class who will not identify herself as a girl. Her parents allow her to dress as a boy (all the way down to underwear), hair cut like a boy, etc. The mother is an alcoholic, and when her dad came to conference, he strongly suggested that the male figure in the family was certainly better to be identified with and just brushed it off as okay. What would you do with this situation now? All of her friends are boys, and they are willing to accept her as one yet at this age.

71. You have just completed an introduction to the female reproductive system in the third day of a sexuality unit for junior high students. At the end

of class, a student approaches you with a request to speak to you during study period or after school. She is hesitant and seems anxious as she speaks. When she returns after school, she is shaking and in tears. She informs you she believes she is pregnant and she does not know what to do. She fears her father may "throw her out of the house" as he did an older sister who was pregnant, so she "cannot tell them!" Her mother also "feared her father." She says her boyfriend says it's her problem." She is a seventh grade student, somewhat shy, from a conservative community and strong religious area, who is emotionally upset, almost uncontrollably. What do you do as a teacher?

72. I was supervising a lunch period during dismissal time when a little seventh grade girl named Sophie asked me if I would get her a rice krispie bar from Sandy, an eighth grader, who had taken it from her. I called to Sandy who was walking ahead of us and asked about the rice krispie bar. She denied having it and then turned on Sophie saying, "I'll kill you, you little bitch!" Then she grabbed Sophie by the hair and slammed her head into a window in the hallway. I yelled, "Sandy, let go of her!" Then she turned toward me, swinging her arm, and screamed, "Shut up, you f---ing bitch!" I felt helpless. Sandy was much bigger than I, and with the anger in her face, I feared she would hit me if I touched her. I also feared for Sophie. When Sandy turned to confront me, Sophie managed to get away and we started running together down the hall. Sandy continued to pursue both of us, grabbing at Sophie's hair and swearing at us. A male teacher interceded and forced Sandy to walk in the opposite direction. Sophie and I went to the principal's office to report the incident. We were both in tears and Sophie's head hurt. Two days later, I filed a deposition at the police station against Sandy for her assault. She was suspended from school for two weeks.

73. The latest prank in the junior high is giving a "swirley." No one really wants a swirley, but, by force, a student may get one. A "swirley" is when a group captures another student and takes him/her into the boys' lavatory and puts his/her head under a flushing urinal or in a flushing toilet. What would you do if a student came to you and said he/she had to change clothes because he/she was wet from just getting a "swirley?"

74. The first day of my eighth grade home economics class, I was told by one of the boys, "My dad doesn't think home ec. is important for boys, so I don't have to do much of anything in this class!" Needless to say, I wasn't anticipating this.

75. One day as I was walking down the hall, I heard a voice behind me say, "Pink--yuck! Pink is ugly! She's in pink. She's ugly." I turned around to see a group of my eighth grade boys snickering and looking in my direction. (I was wearing a pink outfit that day.)

76. A student disgustedly exclaimed, "We never had to do this kind of assignment for last year's teacher, Mrs. X . . . !!" and glared at me very pointedly.

77. We have a teacher in our school whose sight is quite bad. The students are aware of this and take advantage. Another English teacher and I have classes in his room following his classes. We are amazed at what we find on the walls of this room when we enter. Most of the time, it is a <u>Playboy</u> centerfold. He cannot see this being done, is totally unaware, and we could not find out who was doing it. I suspect most of the class has a hand in this behavior.

78. The classroom is so noisy next door, your students are complaining they can't concentrate or hear. What should you do?

79. One of the seventh grade boys is always being picked on. He tries to get along with others by giving them gum, candy, or buying a can of pop. He wants to "buy" their friendship. He tells stories of the great things he has done or the great things he can do. Then the others want him to prove the stories he tells. When he can't or doesn't, they proceed to pick on him more, so he tries to give them things again to gain their friendship.

80. The school has a policy of not letting students leave class for the bathroom. One day, in your ninth grade class, you are covering some points on a chart with your class. You notice a small disturbance between two girls in the back of the room. It looks as if one is encouraging the other to raise her hand and get my attention. I asked the one who seemed to be having the problem if anything was wrong.

121

She shook her head no. An assignment was given for the rest of the class period. As I moved around the room to possibly help some students, I noticed one of them sitting in a pool of blood. I quickly told the other one to help her to the nurse. The girl had started to have a miscarriage.

81. One incident in my room involved plagiarism. A freshman paper on herpes looked remarkedly similar to another student's health paper from the previous quarter. A third student told me that the freshman girl, Sarah, had the original paper (Deb's) in her folder. I told this girl to get the paper out of Sarah's folder without Sarah's knowledge, and I made a copy of it and put it back. I was going to confront the girl after school, but she skipped her next hour. Meanwhile, the rest of the class soon learned that I had the "goods" on Sarah. Later that evening, Sarah's mother called me at home. She was extremely upset because she had heard through the grapevine that Sarah was going to flunk for the quarter. I had talked to Sarah's mother at Parent-Teacher conferences about other cheating reported by the students. She told me I had acted very unprofessionally by letting "our little problem" out of the bag. She was going to call the principal and the school board. I told her that was fine with me, and that I wanted to meet with her and go through the two papers together. Sarah's mother came in late that night and admitted there were similarities in the papers, but that they were not identical, so it wasn't copied. Even though the papers were identical in structure, the mother saw nothing wrong. After talking to the principal, I gave Sarah the option of a new topic, which she took. I was upset by the entire thing. Next year, I'll see Sarah every day in class and as an athlete.

BIBLIOGRAPHY

Alschuler, Alfred S. School Discipline, A Socially
    Literate Solution. New York, NY: McGraw-Hill
    Book Company, 1980.

American Federation of Teachers. Discipline--What for
    and How? Chicago, IL: American Federation of
    Teachers, 1957.

Baker, Keith, and Robert J. Rubel. Violence and Crime
    in the Schools. Lexington, MA: D.C. Heath and
    Company, 1980.

Beecher, Marguerite, and Willard Beecher. Parents on
    the Run, A Common Sense Book for Today's Parents.
    New York, NY: Grosset and Dunlap, 1967.

Berne, Eric. Games People Play. New York, NY:
    Ballantine Books, 1964.

Canfield, Jack, and Harold C. Wells. 100 Ways to
    Enhance Self-Concept in the Classroom. Englewood
    Cliffs, NJ: Prentice-Hall, Inc., 1976.

Canter, Lee, with Marlene Canter. Assertive
    Discipline--A Take-Charge Approach for Today's
    Educator. Santa Monica, CA: Canter and Asso.,
    Inc., 1976.

Carducci, Dewey J., and Judith B. Carducci. The
    Caring Classroom, A Guide for Teachers Troubled
    by the Difficult Student and Classroom
    Disruption. Palo Alto, CA: Bull Publishing
    Company, 1984.

Charles, C.M. Building Classroom Discipline. 3rd
    edition. New York, NY: Longman, 1989.

Community Board Program, Inc. (The). The Community
    Conflict Resolution Training Manual. San
    Francisco, CA: The Community Board Center for
    Policy and Training, 1984.

Connors, Eugene T. Student Discipine and the Law.
    Fastback 121. Bloomington, IN: Phi Delta Kappa,
    1979.

Coulby, David, and Tim Harper. Preventing Classroom Disruption--Policy, Practice, and Evaluation in Urban Schools. Dover, NH: Croom Helm, 1985.

Cummings, Carol. Managing to Teach. Edmonds, WA: Teaching, Inc., 1983.

Dinkmeyer, Don, and Gary D. McKay. The Parent's Guide, Step/Teen--Systematic Training for Effective Parenting of Teens. Circle Pines, MN: American Guidance Service, 1983.

Dinkmeyer, Don, Gary D. McKay, and Don Dinkmeyer, Jr. STET--Systematic Training for Effective Teaching, Leader's Manual. Circle Pines, MN: American Guidance Services, Inc., 1980.

Dobson, James. The Strong-Willed Child, Birth through Adolescence. Wheaton, IL: Tyndale House Publishers, Inc., 1978.

---. Dare to Discipline. Wheaton, IL: Tyndale House Publishers, Inc., 1970.

Dreikurs, Rudolf. Psychology in the Classroom. 2nd edition. New York: Harper and Row, Publishers, Inc., 1957, 1968.

---. Social Equality: The Challenge of Today. Chicago, IL: Contemporary Books, Inc., 1971.

Dreikurs, Rudolf, with Vicki Soltz. Children: The Challenge. New York, NY: Hawthorn/Dutton, 1964.

Dreikurs, Rudolf, and Pearl Cassell. Discipline without Tears. 2nd edition. New York: Hawthorn/ Dutton, 1972.

Duke, Daniel L., and Adrienne M. Meckel. Teacher's Guide to Classroom Management. New York, NY: Random House, Inc., 1984.

Emmer, Edmund T., Carolyn M. Evertson, Julie P. Sanford, Barbara S. Clements, and Murray E. Worsham. Organizing and Managing the Junior High Classroom. Austin, TX: The Research and Development Center for Teacher Education, The University of Texas at Austin (R&D Rep. No. 6151).

Englander, Meryl E. Strategies for Classroom Discipline. Westport, CT: Greenwood Press, 1986.

Ernst, Ken. Games Students Play (and What to Do about Them). Millbrae, CA: Celestial Arts, 1972.

Ezer, Melvin. Training Manual for School Mediation. Honolulu, HI: Department of Educational Foundations, College of Education, University of Hawaii.

Foster, Herbert L. Ribbin', Jivin', and Playin' the Dozens--The Unrecognized Dilemma of Inner City Schools. Cambridge, MA: Ballinger Publishing Company, 1974.

Freed, Alvyn M. T.A. for Teens (and Other Important People). Sacramento, CA: Jalmar Press, Inc., 1976.

George, Paul S. Classroom Discipline and Contingency Management. Gainesville, FL: Teacher Education Resources, Inc., 1979.

Glasser, William. Control Theory in the Classroom. New York, NY: Harper and Row, Publishers, Inc., 1985.

---. Reality Therapy, A New Approach to Psychiatry. New York, NY: Harper and Row, Publishers, Inc., 1965.

Gordon, Thomas. T.E.T.--Teacher Effectiveness Training. New York, NY: David McKay, Inc., 1974.

Gouldner, Helen. Teachers' Pets, Troublemakers, and Nobodies--Black Children in Elementary School. Westport, CT: Greenwood Press, Inc., 1978.

Grossnickle, Donald R., and Frank P. Sesko. Promoting Effective Discipline in School and Classroom. Reston, VA: National Association of Secondary School Principals, 1985.

Handy, John. Involvement Therapy--A Treatment Model Developed at the Minnesota Correctional Facility. Red Wing, MN.

Hauck, Paul A. The Rational Management of Children. Roslyn Heights, NY: Libra Publishers, Inc., 1967.

Hotchkiss, Lawrence. Effects of Schooling on Cognitive, Attitudinal, and Behavioral Outcomes. Columbus, OH: The National Center for Research in Vocational Education--The Ohio State University, 1984.

Jones, Vernon F. Adolescents with Behavior Problems--Strategies for Teaching, Counseling, and Parent Involvement. Boston, MA: Allyn and Bacon, Inc., 1980.

Kohut, Sylvester, Jr., and Dale G. Range. Classroom Discipline: Case Studies and Viewpoints. Washington, D.C.: National Education Association, 1979.

Kounin, Jacob S. Discipline and Group Management in Classrooms. New York, NY: Holt, Rinehart and Winston, Inc., 1970.

Kvols-Riedler, Bill, and Kathy Kvols-Riedler. Redirecting Children's Misbehavior. Boulder, CO: R.D.I.C. Publications, 1979.

Long, James D., and Robert L. Williams. SOS for Teachers, Strategies of Self-Improvement. Princeton, NJ: Princeton Book Company, Publishers, 1982.

Lundell, Kerth T. Levels of Discipline, A Complete System for Behavior Management in the Schools. Springfield, IL: Charles C. Thomas, Publisher, 1982.

Martin, Garry, and Joseph Pear. Behavior Modification, What It Is and How to Do It. Englewood Cliffs, NJ: Prentice-Hall, Inc., 1983.

McCarthy, Susan P., and Edward O. Brown. "Catch 'Em Being Good." Seattle, WA: Center for Law and Justice, University of Washington, 1983.

Medland, Michael, and Michael Vitale. Management of Classrooms. New York, NY: Holt, Rinehart and Winston, 1984.

National Education Association. Discipline in the Classroom--The Least Approach. Washington, D.C.: National Education Association, 1980.

---. _Discipline Dilemma_. Washington, D.C.: National Education Association (Stock No. 1514-2-00).

National Institute of Education. _Violent Schools-- Safe Schools, The Safe School Study Report to the Congress_, Volume 1. Washington, D.C.: U.S. Department of Health, Education, and Welfare, Jan. 1978.

National School Boards Association. _Toward Better and Safer Schools, A School Leader's Guide to Delinquency Prevention_. Alexandria, VA: National School Boards Association, 1984.

National School Safety Center. _School Discipline Notebook_. Sacramento, CA: Pepperdine University Press and the National School Safety Center, 1986.

Rich, H. Lyndall. _Disturbed Students--Characteristics and Educational Strategies_. Baltimore, MD: University Park Press, 1982.

Rivers, L. Wendell. _The Disruptive Student and the Teacher_. Washington, D.C.: National Education Association, 1977.

Rubel, Robert J. _Dealing with Rotten Kids in Schools: An Examination of Options_. Austin, TX: National Alliance for Safe Schools, 1979.

---. _The Unruly School_. Lexington, MA: D.C. Heath and Company, 1977.

Rubel, Robert J., and Nancy L. Ames. _Reducing School Crime and Student Misbehavior: A Problem-Solving Strategy_. Washington, D.C.: U.S. Department of Justice, National Institute of Justice--Office of Development, Testing, and Dissemination, March 1985.

Sanford, Julie P., and Edmund T. Emmer. _Understanding Classroom Management_. Englewood Cliffs, NJ: Prentice-Hall, Inc., 1988.

Sheviakov, George V., and Fritz Redl. _Discipline for Today's Children and Youth_. Washington, D.C.: Association for Supervision and Curriculum Development, 1944, 1956.

Silvermann, Marvin. How to Handle Problem Behaviors in School. Lawrence, KS: H & H Enterprises, Inc., 1980.

Southwest Texas State University. Classroom Management and Discipline Program Manual--A Modular Text. San Marcos, TX: Classroom Management and Discipline Program, Lyndon B. Johnson Institute for the Improvement of Teaching and Learning, School of Education, 1987.

Sprick, Randall S. Discipline in the Secondary School, A Problem-by-Problem Survival Guide. West Nyack, NY: The Center for Applied Research in Education, Inc., 1985.

Stainback, Susan B., and William C. Stainback. Classroom Discipline, A Positive Approach. Springfield, IL: Charles C. Thomas, Publisher, 1974.

Stark, Rodney. Religion and Delinquency: The Ecology of a "Lost" Relationship. Seattle, WA: Center for Law and Justice, University of Washington, 1979.

Swick, Kevin J. Maintaining Productive Student Behavior. Washington, D.C.: National Education Association, 1977.

Vorrath, Harry H. Positive Peer Culture--Content, Structure, and Process. Red Wing, MN: Minnesota State Training School for Boys.

Wallen, Carl J., and LaDonna L. Wallen. Effective Classroom Management. Boston, MA: Allyn and Bacon, Inc., 1978.

Wolfgang, Charles H., and Carl D. Glickman. Solving Discipline Problems--Strategies for Classroom Teachers. Boston, MA: Allyn and Bacon, Inc., 1980.

Zirkel, Perry A. A Digest of Supreme Court Decisions Affecting Education. Bloomington, IN: Phi Delta Kappa, 1982.

ABOUT THE AUTHOR

Robert L. Major, Professor of Curriculum and Instruction at Mankato State University, supervises student teachers and teaches undergraduate and graduate courses, including Discipline and Classroom Management, Discipline: Current Models, Preventive Discipline and School Discipline.

Born and raised in western Nebraska, with a mother who was a school teacher, Dr. Major began his career teaching secondary social studies and English in his native state. He earned graduate degrees in education at the University of Nebraska--Lincoln, Teachers College Columbia University, and the University of Northern Colorado.

A teacher educator for the past 20 years, Dr. Major has served as co-director of the Center for Personal Development in Teaching at MSU, studied at the National School Safety Center in Los Angeles, and at the National Office of Juvenile Justice and Delinquency Prevention in Washington, D.C. He has conducted post-doctoral research as a visiting scholar at the University of Wisconsin--Madison and at the University of California--Berkeley.

This book is his first. It has been preceded by over two dozen published articles and book reviews, and the raising of three sons to adulthood.